POSITIVE PSYCHOLOGY IN WAR-TRAUMA THERAPY

BY DRAGAN MIRKOVIĆ

Title of the original (German) publication:

"POSITIVE PSYCHOLOGIE IN DER KRIEGSTRAUMA-THERAPIE"
published by Create Space and Amazon Kindle

Copyright © 2012, 2014 by Dragan Mirković

Publisher: CREATE SPACE,
DBA of On-Demand Publishing LLC
is a part of the Amazon group of companies

Date of publication: July 2014

Disclaimers Warranties

Cover page designed by the author
Layout designed by the author

ISBN-13: 978-1500390969
ISBN-10: 1500390968

POSITIVE PSYCHOLOGY IN WAR-TRAUMA THERAPY

INTEGRATION OF POSITIVE PSYCHOLOGY WITH WAR TRAUMA THERAPY AND CHRISTIAN PASTORAL CARE

Most of the material is taken from the master's thesis
with the same title in German

In order to obtain the academic degree
Master of Arts (M.A.)

Submitted
by

Dragan Mirković
Friedensau, July 2012

First reviewer: Andreas Bochmann, Ph.D. (USA)
Second reviewer: Prof. Dr. Phil. Thomas Steininger

ACKNOWLEDGEMENTS

Above all, the greatest thanks belongs to my first reviewer and teacher, Andreas Bochmann, Ph.D., without whose support, this very valuable study would not have been possible for me. My sincere gratitude for this work also belongs to my second reviewer and supervisor Prof. Dr. phil. Thomas Steininger and also to the Dipl.-Psych. Wolfgang Schwabe and my supervisor, also to graduate social worker, Dagmar Jansen (MA. Counseling), for their intellectual support and guidance. Especially great thank belongs to my wife Snežana, who has supported me in my studies all the time.

ABSTRACT

This research deals with a completely new combination of positive psychology, war trauma therapy and Christian pastoral care in the treatment of post-traumatic stress. Since war trauma stress affects both civilians and soldiers coming from the war affected areas, this work is devoted to both those groups. These include also German citizens who are traumatized from the 2nd world war. The goal of this research is to integrate the values and methods of positive psychology with pastoral care of war traumatized people.

Key words: trauma, war trauma, posttraumatic stress disorder, resilience, positive psychology, recovery and growth, spirituality, pastoral care.

CONTENTS

1. INTRODUCTION

About 80 percent of people endure in their lifetime at least one traumatic event, but without permanent consequences (Michels Kliniken, 2008). In the Western population suffer still 10 percent of people at least once in the life of trauma-related mental disorder (Michels Kliniken, 2008; Jossen, 2007). The experience leaves especially strong trauma-related mental traces, not only in the war-generation but also in their offspring (Ermann, 2003). Although the war is almost over 62 years,

> ...There are the traces of the second world that still not faded in our country [...], it is nevertheless post-war period. The confrontation with nationalism, the second world war and its consequences determines our political, social and cultural life" (Ermann, 2003).

Wars are apparently continued. The signs are visible not only through numerous human sacrifices, but also through the lives of the survivors. The venomous cycle doesn't just end here. The trauma affects not only the victims, but also indirectly their children and sometimes even their grand children. War trauma involves lifelong consequences. This research focuses on the following research objectives with this in mind (the following chapter).

This book is a translation from the original German work with the same title on German: "Positive Psychologie in Der Kriegstrauma Therapie". All German citations are also translated to English.

1.1. Clarification of the Research Concern

The need for discussion of the subject of trauma growth – We live in a world full of tension, changes and incisive war experiences. These concern not only the financial and the political world, but also the life of each individual through:

> "... war, natural disasters, accidents, fires and interpersonal violence (for example, sexual violence). Individuals, families or entire communities may be affected. People may lose their homes or loved ones, be separated from family and community, or may witness violence, destruction or death" (World Health Organization, 2011, p. 2).

The mental trauma and damage afterwards is enormous and devastating, in many cases so much that the whole worldview and attitude toward life is completely changed. The value estimation, self-esteem and basic attitude to life are often heavily damaged. Especially in cases of the experience of violence and death of the beloved persons is the suffering on the one hand very deep; on the other hand are anger and hatred against perpetrators are so strong, that these negative feelings and thoughts can completely change a person.[1]

Not only personal damage arising therefrom, but often dealing of such a traumatized person with their living environment is so negative and in some cases destructive. The consequences of that are felt then by all the people who are in

---

[1] A common conclusion trough several conversations with war traumatized people: "If you come from the war you are a completely different person"

their environment. If many people are affected, subsequently the whole society is influenced. Therefore the efficiency of the counseling by qualitative approaches is important to restrain apparently increasing and difficult mental stress.

There are new resource-oriented approaches in the praxis. The standardized illness-healing orientation in clinical psychotherapy and counseling, which deals with dislikable symptoms (Joseph & Linley, 2008), is no longer enough for a constructive resistance force of advice seekers, to be able to cope with constantly new life challenges. It is of outstanding importance to learn survival strategies, to be able to master permanent life changes and permanently to maximize the quality of life.

Positive psychology, a new resource-oriented psychology discipline since August 21th 1999 (Joseph & Linley, 2008) deals not especially with ill and negative mental states, as in the long-established and standardized clinical psychotherapy, but rather with facing positive skills and qualities of life – resilience, happiness, joy, hope, satisfaction. The development of positive relationships, basic attitudes, structures and life values helps to improve life (Joseph & Linley, 2008). The research of positive psychology in recent years in the field of posttraumatic disorders (Linley & Joseph, 2004b; Seligman & Csikszentmihalyi, 2000; Snyder & Lopez, 2002, cited in Joseph & Linley, 2008) is a further contribution of trauma war therapy. After such extensive research, it seems to me, as a pastor, that the approach of the Positive psychology, along with other solution- and resource-oriented psychotherapy- and counseling-methods, is very useful and rewarding. These positive approaches are not foreign even for Christian values of pastoral care, which are necessary especially in difficult phases of life. Therefore, in this context, it is useful to find the answers to the following questions:

- What has proven itself in the practice of psychotherapy and pastoral care that has helped people with such a serious experience, not only to free them from the negative aftereffects, but rather to develop something positive, to grow and to be even more mature?

- What has protected such people of introjection, not to be transformed from victims to offenders?

- What has helped them in the therapeutic practice to gain positive values of humanity, dignity, love and hope and consequently to improve the quality of their lives?

- How to empower counselors and pastoral ministers to help such people more effectively and better?

These are just a few questions that this study deals with directly and indirectly. This research is illuminated from two aspects, which I consider as very important and suitable for this problem:

- on the one hand – from the point of view of Positive psychology and

- on the other hand from the point of view of Christian pastoral care.

This is addressed in particular with these issues:

- in which extent are these approaches compatible with each other and how to distinguish them?

- how can you both effectively apply in the war trauma therapy, as in the counseling and also in the pastoral care of such people and integrate both with each other?

- In all these efforts of trying to help such traumatized people, it is important to include also their environment.

Although each study keeps consistently to its logic and discipline, this work is comprehensive, covering the psychotherapeutic, counseling and pastoral aspects. The main objective of this study will finally be apparent. Therefore, this book is dedicated to all three groups of social experts.

1.2. Subject of War Trauma

War trauma is an old but very real problem. A quite problematic burden for many people today in Germany, Europe and worldwide is war trauma. Many older generations are affected also here in Germany (Gestrich, 2005). Although the World War II has passed long ago, its long-term effects are still deeply set – not only in the generations that were born before and during the war, but also in their children and even grandchildren (Gestrich, 2005; Ermann, 2003).[2] It influences also society as a whole. The following data demonstrate this reality:

After the Second World War, 200.000 children in Germany have lost both parents, 2.5 Millions have one parent and more than one third have experienced escape and expulsion (Gestrich, 2005). Today they are 60-75-year-old

---

[2] Originally, all details are mentioned on the Congress "The generation of war children and their village for Europe" in Frankfurt am Main on April 14th 2005 – April 16th 2005.

Germans out of which only 30 % are not affected from war trauma, 30% of them are averagely damaged and 40% seriously damaged (Gestrich, 2005). The consequences of such trauma are often repeated and chronic:

> "Diseases, disabilities, injuries, mutilation and nutritional deficiencies. Psychological consequences are agitation and nervousness, emotional liability, fear of contact, depression, specific fears and stress disorders (in particular post-traumatic stress disorder). In social areas, the children exhibit a pronounced inappropriate social behavior, increased aggressiveness, a distorted understanding of morality and a cognitive adaptation to their violent, threatening environment" (Albrecht, 2001, p. 2).

Trauma affects not only the affected ones, it will continue on their children and relatives through the transfer of the so-called secondary traumatization (Gestrich, 2005). The tragedy is, that not infrequently, a transfer of the «ethical» values from the offender to the victim (introjection) takes place, in turn to make themselves into new offenders – so called «Offender Introjection» (Michels Kliniken, 2008). The vicious circle is thus opened.

This is not only a reality of the past. In psychotherapy and counseling in recent decades many refugees and immigrants come with symptoms of the war trauma from various world regions that have been affected by war (Lanfranchi, 2004). Some of them may be mentioned: former Yugoslavia, Iraq, Afghanistan, Africa, etc. Also more and more Federal German army soldiers seek help, who struggle after returning from the battlefield with severe post-traumatic stress disorder (PTSD) (Bundes Psychotherapeuten Kammer,

2012; Naumann, 2009; Joseph & Linley, 2008; Jossen, 2007), often accompanied by a variety of other mental disorders (Michels Kliniken, 2008). Their special needs and problems require special treatment. In addition to that, many people from the former East Germany have experienced war-related trauma in a totalitarian regime after the Second World War (Bundeszentrale für politische Bildung, 2003). If the consequences of crime are also counted, which is very often similar to war trauma (IRP-HSG, 2012), the need is always after the effective up-to-date counseling, therapy and pastoral approaches.

In the context of war trauma therapy and positive psychology, the following questions arise in this work:

• How can be contributed to war-traumatized people with the help of positive psychology, to develop new positive life qualities and values in their lives?

• What approaches are the most applicable in such cases?

• To what extent has positive psychology been proven in war trauma therapy?

In the context of the comparison of positive psychology with other approaches, additional questions arise:

• To what extent are approaches and assumptions of positive psychology available in other resource-oriented therapy / counseling approaches and methods?

• Which contribution brings positive psychology to other modern therapy / counseling approaches in war trauma therapy?

As a Christian counselor, I also deal with the following questions:

- To what extent, on the basis of the contemporary scientific point of view, is positive psychology compatible with Christian faith and Christian pastoral care?

- How can Christian pastoral care give a reasonable explanation for the injustice that has affected trauma victims?

- How can Christian values, alongside with positive psychology, bring back the life dignity and the life meaning to war-traumatized people?

- Finally, how can the quality of life be enriched and improved with the help of Positive psychology and Christian pastoral care together?

The aim of this study is to give a useful contribution and treatment maxims to psychotherapists, counselors and pastors in their work, as well as to the life of traumatized people. However, to achieve that, this study needs further deepening.

1.3. Personal Interests for the Theme's Choice

Through the background from a country that was affected by a series of civil wars through a whole decade, I know through my own experience how a war seems to be and which consequences arise from it. In the time of civil wars in Slovenia, Croatia, Bosnia and Herzegovina all that could be seen every day almost a decades long on live TV programs. Finally, air strikes in Serbia, Kosovo and Montenegro have left deep traces in our memory and in the souls of our whole family. During the recent war in Serbia and Montenegro, our daily agenda included alarm sirens that were often louder than bombs themselves and very often seeking escape and a safe refuge from bombs. During the night bombing, we had to hide always our children in a "safe room" to avoid any shrapnel. Sometimes by driving through destroyed fields and cities we have such overwhelming experiences, as we had to behold these scenes of devastation and destruction, that we were stunned and sometimes even crying. Our children had to experience strong fears and horrors by air attacks that have left a deep trauma, also several years after the war. Likewise here in Germany they have cried almost always when they heard fireworks or aircraft flying. Health problems of our children and subsequent extensive investigations were an additional burden and consequences of war.

As a result of all of that, for me as a pastor and counselor, it is easy to understand how war affects people and how to put myself in their situation. Finally, empathy is a task that each man and Christian can reach, what Apostle Paul wrote from personal experience:

> 2 Corinthians [1.3] "Praise be to God the father of our Lord Jesus, Christ, the father of mercies and God of all consolation, [1.4] who comforts us in all our tribulation so that we also can take comfort that are in all sorts of affliction, with the comfort with which we ourselves are comforted by God" (Luther's Bible, 1996 translated from German).

Many people in need of pastoral care come to the limits of understanding, especially in such difficult situations of suffering, to the question: "Why has a loving Heavenly Father allowed it? Why so much suffering and injustice, if he is omnipotent?"

Yet, rather than just only asking, practical answers and solutions are required. Therapeutic action is necessary both by those affected and with the help of their relatives. On the one hand, **psychology** can help to illuminate scientifically the positive content of pastoral care. These psychological models help to bridge and to expand the boundaries of pastoral care. On the other hand, **faith** and **hope** can give a higher sense to life, what is the basic need of every human. Therefore, a combination of both approaches is enriching.

This research is a literary work, because the research in the positive psychology is, especially here in Europe, in the process of development. A combination of positive psychology with Christian pastoral care is even rarely – actually not yet been developed. Therefore, this work is a pioneering work on the concept of integration of these two approaches in trauma treatment. Furthermore, the combination of positive and clinical psychotherapy is also complementary to each other to enrich all dimension of psychotherapy.

2. EXPLANATION OF THE USED TERMS AND DEFINITIONS

In trauma therapy, some terms in the professional terminology are used by default. However, some items in positive psychology are differently understood and interpreted. This difference is evident in the following chapters. At the same time Christian view will also be represented in the context of trauma.

2.1. Trauma

The main concept and the main problem, which this research is dealing with, is trauma. The word comes from the Greek word *"to trauma"* and means "wound" (Bauer, 1971, p. 1631) or "infringement".

> "The field of Psychotraumatology deals with the formation, acquisition, history and treatment of psychological injuries, that come as a result of extremely more burdensome or life-threatening events (Landlot, 2004)" (Landlot & Hensel, 2008, p. 14).

Klessmann makes the definition of trauma in his work "Seelsorge" ("Pastoral Care") as follows:

> "A traumatic event may refer to a stressful event or a situation of exceptional threat or catastrophic scale (short or long-lasting), which was causing deep despair in almost every case. The discrepancy between experienced threat and coping resources is crucial for the extent of the trauma. So

you cannot objectively measure trauma, it depends on the subjective perception or assessment." (Klessmann, 2008, p. 294).

Another definition describes trauma as:

> "Objective, sudden, short or long-lasting or recurring, existentially threatening and inescapable event outside the normal human experience standard, which raises the subjective experience of absolute helplessness, powerlessness, intense fear and horror.
> In the definition of trauma, experience of intense fear and horror, of absolute helplessness and powerlessness are explicitly noticeable" (Zahlner, 2008, p. 1).

Although every unpleasant experience can be understood individually as trauma, the following symptoms of a trauma must be met:

> "Recurrent, sudden memories of the event in nightmares or so-called flash-backs, which, as the term says, overwhelms the person, so that he/she cannot distance themselves from that; also in the expressing of the event can such a flooding and thus a kind of re-trauma takes place – the narrative should be interrupted if necessary (Klessmann, 2008, p. 294f).

Of all people who have experienced one or more traumatic events only some of them become traumatized and ill. Not all people who have the experience of a war become mentally and health affected. The majority of them live a long-term completely normal life. What does actually cause post-traumatic stress in this minority who cannot manage it as others do?

"The characteristics of traumatic situations determine the risk significantly. Especially the factors as age at the beginning of the trauma, duration of exposure, experiences of interpersonal violence in contrast to disasters and strokes of fate, the nature of the relationship to the perpetrator and the resulting physical damage are of crucial significance" (Michels Kliniken, 2008, p. 4).

To avoid unpleasant memories, traumatized people develop an avoidance strategy in their behavior and a general emotional state of numbness (Gehring, 2010; Michels Kliniken, 2008), and even lasting overexcitation (Gehring, 2010; Michels Kliniken, 2008).

Trauma disorders are very complex. There are different causes and types of them.

2.1.1. Typological Classification of the Trauma

Trauma can be classified according to several types. For example on the cause type:

Type 1 [Mono Trauma (Seidler, Freyberger, & Maercker, 2011, p. 180)]

> • "[...] human caused, in the short term
> • e.g. road accidents, short-lasting disasters (hurricane, fire)
> • sexual assault
> • criminal, physical violence
> • civilian violence experience (robbers) " (Gehring, 2010, p. 5).

Type 2 ["repeated trauma in the context of a close relationship structure" (Seidler, Freyberger, & Maercker, 2011, p. 180)]

- "in the long term
- e.g. long-lasting natural disasters (earthquake, flood)
- sex/physical violence in childhood
- war experience
- hostage, torture
- political detention" (Gehring, 2010, p. 6).

There is also a classification of **duration** and **scope**:

"In addition to the one time trauma, multiple trauma and complex trauma are made also other categorizations:

Cumulative trauma (sequential trauma): a consequence of a series of traumatic experiences, which lead to the collapse of the mental structure;

Childhood trauma / Adolescent trauma: This categorization is urgently needed. The "developmental trauma succession disorder" conceptualized in recent times represents a new diagnostic category and will be included in the next period in the ICD 10 and DSM IV" (Zahlner, 2008, p. 1).

"Individual vs. collective trauma: [...] Angwyn St. Just represents a practicable approach for "social trauma therapy". This method integrates the possibilities that arise from the combination of the systemic perspective with somatic trauma work, especially with regard to the area of the social/global trauma. Also intergenerational trauma is an issue for systemic trauma work.

A possible categorization is also the description of so-called **'big- T-trauma'**, experiences of existential external or internal threat of violence, threat of violence on the body such as physical and sexual abuse, mental cruelty and severe mistreatment by close, familiar people, moreover, if the trauma begins to occur repeatedly over long periods of time very early in childhood, if it could never be expressed and if they never experienced protection or comfort. To that belong other criminal attacks on the body, on the life and on the emotional or social existence, terror and torture experience in military, political and criminal contexts, nature- and transport disasters, accidents, severe disease, sudden loss of close friends and family.

As **'small-t-Trauma'** is described as less catastrophic events, which accompanied with fright and fear in connection with a high degree of disturbing humiliation, embarrassment, deep uncertainty and with the same inevitability as the big trauma happened to those affected.

The causes of trauma can be divided according to Peter Levine in obvious and subtle.

Peter Levine uses also the categorization according to the respective cause of trauma for the SE-specific treatment" (Zahlner, 2008, p. 1).

Although the term "trauma" and "traumatic" in everyday speech are often used carelessly, a distinction between "stressful life events and traumatic events" should be made (Michels Kliniken, 2008, p. 4).

"An event or situation is only referred to as "psychological trauma", when from it comes an outstanding threat, or if it reaches a catastrophic level and at the same time is accompanied by intense fear, experience of helplessness or scaring. Traumatic events threaten the physical or mental integrity, the life" (Michels Kliniken, 2008, p. 4).

Like for all mental disorders and diseases, also for trauma, there exists a clear medical diagnosis.

2.1.2. Medical Classification of Traumas

Trauma as "Acute stress disorder, F 43.0" is defined according to ICD-10. However it includes many different comorbid (combined) disorder modes:

"The post traumatic stress disorder is a specific form of a trauma following disturbance. With it the following disorders are related:

Acute stress reaction ICD10: F 43.0

Adjustment disorder ICD10: F 43.2

Ongoing personality changes after extreme stress ICD10: F 62.0.

The extensive consequences of personality development impaired by trauma, are currently under the terms "complex traumatic stress disorder", "developmental trauma disorder" or discussed "complex presentation of a post-traumatic disorder".

Other trauma consequent disorders are:

- Dissociative disorder images F 44
- Somatoform pain disorder F 45.4
- Emotionally unstable personality disorder (borderline) F 60.3

Other disorders significantly involving traumatic stress are:

- Dissocial personality disorder F 60.2 km
- Eating disorders F 50
- Affective disorders F 32, 33, 34
- Substance dependence F 1
- Somatoform disorders F 45" (AWMF - Fachgesellschaften, 2011, p. 2).

According to the classification of the Diagnostic and Statistical Manual of Mental Disorders (DSM-IV) the definition of trauma is a little different:

> "The current definition of trauma according to DSM-IV-TR contains two aspects, that at the same time must be met (Sass et al., 2003): (1) the affected person experiences or observes an event, that goes hand in hand with a serious threat to the physical or mental integrity of self or of others; (2) the response of the affected individual includes intense fear, helplessness, dread, upset or agitated behavior"
> (Landolt & Hensel, 2008, p. 14).

Which neurobiological processes result from a traumatic experience?

2.1.2.1. Psychological and Physical Reactions

In a traumatic situation the psyche reacts (due to fear of the threat, stress, shock, and sometimes collapse – fear of death), as well as the body (physical pain, heart palpitations, etc.), which gives an intense physical **excitation** (Zahlner, 2008). If there is no possibility of escape, those affected experience a **feeling of helplessness** (Zahlner, 2008). When fighting in a danger does not work, it produces an inner and outer **freezing** (ibid.). As a result, the victim is **helplessly delivered** to the offender, or to the traumatic situation (ibid.). Due to the psychological shock a **memory fragmentation** occurs (dissociation) (ibid.).

Due to an emotional overflowing, a productive processing of traumatic experiences is not possible during the traumatic situation (Michels Kliniken, 2008). Mental processes are reduced usually to the survival function and the conscious perception reduces equally selective, limited, incomplete (events, people, time, location and details are consumed) and is partially disabled to reduce the stress feeling (pain and anxiety reduction) (Michels Kliniken, 2008). Many elements of the traumatic events are distorted and alienated even the self-image (Michels Kliniken, 2008). The victim is put under extreme mental stress in a state of emotional and mental torpor (freezing) whereby the neurobiological fear system of the psyche is highly stimulated, thus fear structure occurs in the central nervous system (Michels Kliniken, 2008). This can cause physical symptoms:

> "Long-lasting post traumatic stress can influence the course of physical diseases through the activation of trauma-related stress. This is especially used for cardiovascular diseases and immunological disorders" (AWMF - societies, 2011, p. 2).

The psyche responds to any traumatic situation only at a reduced level of function to be able to survive the emotional flood (ibid.). Emotions are prevented as well:

> "It comes to the permanent increase of activities in amygdala - and hypothalamus that trigger a neurophysiological dysregulation. In patients with post-traumatic stress disorder the level of corticotrophin releasing factor (CRF) in the cerebrospinal fluid is increasing and at the same time there is a reduced cortisol release after stimulation by CRF. The stress regulation of pituitary adrenal axis is massively disrupted. Sufferers experience therefore the constant stress quite a long time and they no

longer have the security, that the threat is over after the end of the trauma" (Michels Kliniken, 2008, p. 5).

Therefore a great uncertainty results. Hence support from social structures is very important to regain the sense of security and protection (ibid.). Consequently, mental torpor can be resolved only through positive experiences and emotions (understanding, care and physical proximity) (Michels Kliniken, 2008). It is therefore very important also to involve the family members of clients, because they actually play the main role in support and in help of adaptation to the new circumstances and situation.

After the dissolution of the emotional tension intensive emotions, traumatic memories – flashbacks and nightmares often come in appearance (Michels Kliniken, 2008). Also the relatives should be informed, so that they may show no false reactions and complicate an already serious situation. In therapy, counseling or pastoral care, it is very important to help the concerned and related ones to accept such responses as "normal" (ibid.). Through the lack of social support and the available help a negative evaluation of the occurring symptoms can complicate the trauma processing, or even block it (ibid.).

The "Horowitz cascade" is suitable to illustrate this and to distinguish between the normal of the pathological reactions, as well as the emergence of various Posttraumatic reactions and pathological conditions:

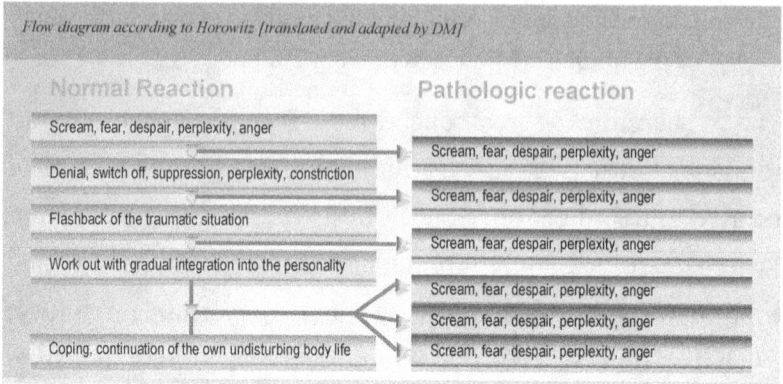

Figure 1 – Normal and Pathologic Reactions
Source: Michels Kliniken, 2008, p. 5

The networking of the whole nerve system with all its organs reflects mental changes in the body – often in the form of somatic or somatoform disorders (Michels Kliniken, 2008). Such disturbances may occur in any organ in the form mainly of pain symptoms, digestive disorders, hypersensitivity and changes on the skin, gynecological complaints, etc. (ibid.). The main connection between the body and the psyche is the autonomic nervous system. Although neurotransmitters (chemical substances communicating between neurons) have a short "life", all sensations and stimuli are stored in the subconscious, primarily in the limbic system, as the body's memory of the traumatic experiences (Michels Kliniken, 2008). Already after an only one traumatic experience, the physical memory is very strong, what can cause all possible somatoform disorders (ibid.). But otherwise, because the perception is fragmented and selective during the traumatic situation, the fragile body feelings in the memory remain without circumstance information of the trauma (Michels Kliniken, 2008). Therefore recurrent somatoform body reactions can be hard to classify – they are very often misinterpreted in the medical diagnosis as organ damage (Michels Kliniken, 2008). That's why it is important in conversation with clients to clarify a causal link between the injury and the somatoform body reactions (ibid.).

2.1.3. War Trauma

Although almost 70 years have passed since the Second World War, its consequences still exist in our society, in politics, but also in many different areas of life (Gestrich, 2005; Ermann, 2003). The "war children" have striven bravely to survive during war circumstances and to cope with them. Very often they claimed: *"we have had no time for a trauma. We had to survive!"*[3] It was most important for them to get through everything. Generations that were born during the war came very early to a "field of silence" and outward unimportance of their war experience. They tried to forsake their biography and life destination in particular about their childhood during the war (Ermann, 2003). It was proved in the psychotherapy of such people due to the fact that in their childhood, a large formative role was played, in which there was hardly a word about the war. There is also hardly any "[...] notable literature, which deals with the trauma and the identity problems of children of war..." (Ermann, 2003, p. 2). Only recently through various meetings and exchanges have war children come sporadically to speak about their war experience (Ermann, 2003). They have been silent a long time and tried to

---

[3] A summary of several conversations with people who have experienced the second world war and also the post-war period. Italics - DM.

block out everything from the war (ibid.). This silence however did not help – the psychological consequences by many of them are still occurring in their dreams and also in the form of mental disorders, but predominantly in the late years of life between 50 and even mid 60's, only in connection with serious symptoms in the psychotherapy (Ermann, 2003). Now are these people in late 70's and 80's.

Many German soldiers, who recently returned from the aforementioned war zones, also suffer from the war trauma and need special treatment.

> "In the past few years the number of soldiers treated for stress disorder multiplied according to the Bundeswehr Ministry of Defense (BMVg). The Bundeswehr Ministry of Defense registered in the past three years – 477 cases of PTSD – a ratio of 0.77 percent. The soldiers were victims of attacks, experienced transport- and mine accidents in Bosnia, Kosovo and Afghanistan, were in hostages or faced other forms of violence. The responses range from sleep disorders via depression to physical infirmities. However, the number of treated cases is not the actual number of those affected after assessment of the Bundeswehr Association. The fear of comrades to come out was great, said Association spokesman Wilfried Stolze. In countries such as Spain, France or Great Britain lie the quota of the traumatized ones about five percent" (Kramer & Birnbaum, 2009).[4]

---

[4] Website:
http://www.tagesspiegel.de/politik/deutschland/behandlungszentrum-kriegstrauma-bilder-die-nicht-vergehen-wollen/1435212.html from February 2nd 2009, seen on the June 26th 2012.

They need special facilities and treatment and are consequently under the responsibility of the military facilities in "[...] Bundeswehr hospitals in Hamburg, Berlin, Koblenz, Ulm and Westerstede and the 14 specialist investigative centers for Psychiatry [...]" (Kramer & Birnbaum, 2009).

Civil treatment and counseling centers are therefore not responsible for the soldiers of the Bundeswehr and the best solution is that they should be referred to a special specialized military facility.

2.1.4. War Experiences

The war trauma is a wide-ranging trauma that can include and exceed all other types of trauma, why those affected experience it during their whole life, what is the reason why it can be never forgotten. The main challenge for both of those affected, as well for therapy, counseling and pastoral care is the way to explore, how to deal with it effectively. Those affected are often traumatized in several ways:

• Through the **experiences of violence** – about 25% of the people affected of war experience (Michels Kliniken, 2008),

• through **captivity** – after a war prisoning comes a serious trauma (PTSD) in approximately 50% of the cases (Michels Kliniken, 2008),

• through **sexual violence** – of all traumatic experiences, sexual rape leaves most the posttraumatic stress disorder – by 60-80% (Michels Kliniken, 2008),

• through the **loss** of family members, friends and often of all possession (Gestrich, 2005).

• This also results in **various other mental disorders**, psychosomatic disorders, dissociative disorders, personality disorders, etc. (Michels Kliniken, 2008).

• Often the following is related to intense fear -, scaring- or strong experience of helplessness (Michels Kliniken, 2008).

In such situations, children often had to become witnesses and victims of violence and suffer extensively. They experience burning cities, wounded bodies and must often spend several days and nights in crowded basements (Gestrich, 2005). Together with adults, they experience deportation and flight, hunger and poverty (ibid.). Many of them lose one or both parents, or siblings (ibid.).

Symptoms of war trauma are largely:

> "Acute reactions of shock, depression and suicide, anxiety and addictions, physical diseases, for which no organic causes could be found, as well as chronic fatigue and insomnia. Especially after combat, where soldiers were critically threatened or comrades died, it may cause PTSD. The experience of an intense fear, helplessness or horror can trigger a severe mental illness months later in which the traumatic event can forever be again uncontrollably experienced (such as nightmares, flashbacks). The normal mental experience is then severely disrupted and for the ill person is much more difficult to lead a normal life again" (Federal psychotherapists Chamber, 2012).[5]

---

[5] Website: http://www.bptk.de/aktuell/einzelseite/artikel/ptbs-risiko.html from April 4th 2012 seen on April 30th 2012.

The consequences of war trauma, its complexity, intensity and duration continue to justify the need for an effective therapy-, consulting- and pastoral methods in order to help to all such people.

The further challenge is immigration. In Germany a more modern issue is added – we live in a multicultural society that leads to mixing of different nationalities in the process of globalization. This brings a great challenge. Many men, women and children have lost their homeland and the fullness of their previous lives (Jossen, 2007). They come to Germany in the hope of being able to start a completely new life. Very often they have abandoned all, or lost, in many cases, not only in material terms, but also their family or family members, their training or education, their job and career (ibid.). They have lost their roots, cultural background and their social support and come to an entirely different, and for them often completely alien world (Jossen, 2007). Not infrequently they know no German and live in state of distress in a highly developed and modernized society. They have big language barriers when dealing daily with people in business, with a doctor, in the environment in the school, on the job, everywhere. Very often they have no proper employment, no training recognized in Germany and therefore no great perspective on life.[6]

One reality cannot be overlooked in trauma therapy: "Migrants have higher impact of symptoms then native patients" (David et al., 2002; Roth, 2007, cited in Jossen, 2007, p. 4); "Asylum seekers have more depression, anxiety

---

[6] Information obtained in the pastoral care of such people.

and PTSD symptoms then other migrants" (Gerritsen et al., 2006, cited in Jossen, 2007, p. 4). In these cases are values particularly in the area of somatization, anxiety and depression are very high (Jossen, 2007). Their post-traumatic stress includes predominantly pain as indication of the nerve-system / body language (ibid.). Thus the main cause of the detected symptom exposure comes much later (Jossen, 2007), similar as it is to the war generation in Germany, who tried, due to the long silence, to fight alone with these symptoms (Gestrich, 2005). They experience their migration as a loss – loss of their social status, loss of family relationships, of their material possessions, uprooting, culture shock and their expectations after migration are often disappointed (Jossen, 2007). These are some of the reasons, why healing from their post-traumatic stress is sometimes almost impossible (ibid.). That's why war-traumatized immigrants are still more burdened than domestic patients (David et al., 2002; Roth, 2007, cited in Jossen, 2007, p. 4). All this causes that work with war trauma to be a very great challenge in the psychotherapy and the counseling.

In addition, the local citizens have also problems: to communicate and to work with such people and to create a suitable social climate. If crime was also included, that leaves also severe traumatizing; the issue of trauma is contemporary and common. This is a reality in our society, which doesn't gradually disappear, but grows through numerous global crises in various areas in the world. That is still not realized enough in the integration process of immigrants. That's why it is important not only in this research, but also generally in the social work and especially in psychotherapy, counseling and pastoral care of such people to ask the following questions:

• What challenges do these people have? Which problems must they cope with?

• How can we help them to be better integrated in our society and as part of it to make a good contribution – with a good education, good social commitment, creativity and also financially with being employed in a well paid (and also taxed) job (Joseph & Linley, 2008)?

2.1.5. Post-traumatic Stress Disorder (PTSD)

The most common disorder of trauma consequences and especially of war trauma following disturbance is the post-traumatic stress disorder (PTSD), which blocks the treating of trauma symptoms (Michels Kliniken, 2008). In addition, the other combined mental problems appear which exceed the criteria of PTSD – comorbidity (combined) mental disorders come often.

The main symptoms of PTSD can be divided into four groups:

1. Intrusion - inner reliving of the trauma. During the traumatic situation there arises a strong emotional excess emotion, a fragmented memory and perception – fragmentation consisting of various fractions of a neurobiological perspective very strongly coded and intensified – **hypermnesia**, where background- and contextual information pass into forgetfulness – **hypomnesia** (Michels Kliniken, 2008). Occasionally comes partial or complete amnesia (memory loss of traumatic events), where the feelings

of anxiety are strongly stimulated (Michels Kliniken, 2008).
Unwanted flashbacks to the traumatic events may occur:

> [...] as images, emotions, thoughts, smells, sounds,
> taste, or as pain or tension on various body parts. These
> fragments often seem to be not related and occur often in
> recurring nightmares"(Michels Kliniken, 2008, p. 6). "

Additionally there is sleepwalking, sleep fighting,
panic attacks and nightmares (Clinton & Hawkins, 2011, p.
403).

2. Avoidance reaction. Because the traumatic
memories are often painfully experienced, they cause negative
emotions – feelings of helplessness, anger, guilt, fear and
shame (Michels Kliniken, 2008). As a result the affected
people take various prevention strategies, not to have to think
about the trauma – 'Safety behavior' – they avoid situations
and places that can cause unpleasant memories (ibid.). Not
infrequently, it causes a retreat from the social environment
and thus an extremely suspicious consideration of other people
(Michels Kliniken, 2008).

3. Constriction – stupor response. To protect
themselves from extreme emotional states (trauma), the
neurobiological regulation system blocks emotional impulses –
adding a feeling of numbness (anhedonia) and sometimes also
a derealization of life and of self (depersonalization) (Michels
Kliniken, 2008; Clinton & Hawkins, 2011). In addition to that
come also self-denial, sadness, feeling of emptiness and
depression (Clinton & Hawkins, 2011).

4. Overexcitation – physical arousal. Fragmented memories of the traumatic events are often accompanied by the unpleasant sensations by strong physical reactions:

> "Common symptoms are heart palpitations, sweating, restlessness, excessive stimulation sensitivity, and sudden reactions of the gastro-intestinal tract. Many sufferers experience a low stress tolerance, sudden anger and an increased irritability, what be explained by the continuing changes in the regulation of stress. Insomnia in the context of post traumatic stress disorder can occur besides nightmares also due to this overexcitation." (Michels Kliniken, 2008, p. 7).

Moreover it can be manifested also as temper outbursts, fear as result of violence, excessive caution, moderately scaring and nightly sweating (Clinton & Hawkins, 2011). To successfully handle these processes, protection and security through social groups are of great help (ibid.). Only then, deeply repressed negative emotions can break out (ibid.). For a better understanding of the complexity of the symptoms, the PTSD consequences can be represented graphically as follows (Figure 2).

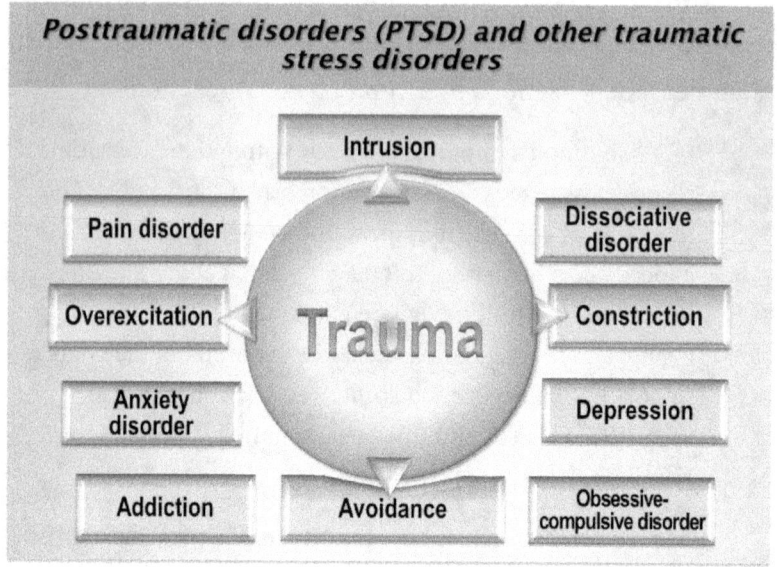

Figure 2: PTSD and other trauma complications
Source: (Michels Kliniken, 2008, p. 7)
[Translated and adapted – DM]

"At multiple, long-lasting traumas in the early life history complex pathological images can be represented. Common symptoms of traumatic stress disorders are:

- Depression

- Persistent somatoform pain disorders

- Dissociative symptoms (depersonalization, derealization,
   pseudo neurological or malposition diseases)

- Anxiety disorders

- Addictions

- Dysregulation of emotions and impulses

- Self-accusation, permanent self-injury or chronic feelings of shame
    - Failure to address sustainable emotional relationships
    - Loss of prior stable values and beliefs" (Michels Kliniken, 2008, p. 7).

From these primary traumatic stress disorders develop **secondary** ones, so called comorbid traumatic stress disorders, for example **agoraphobia** (claustrophobia) as a safekeeping behavior, **addiction** abuse as an escape from the overload of emotion, or **somatoform complaints** as a return of physical memories of traumatic experiences which were very often misinterpreted as a generalized anxiety disorder. The causal relationship between traumatizing cause and comorbid illnesses, or disorder, is mostly only comprehensible through a recording of the whole story in the context of therapy, counseling or pastoral care (Michels Kliniken, 2008). It is important to note that, for some traumatized persons, post-traumatic stress symptoms can occur after years or decades (Michels Kliniken, 2008). Those affected try unnoticed to adapt themselves psychosocially to compensate for the trauma and to overcome it (ibid.).

The whole process of the trauma with its different paths of development can be represented graphically as follows (Figure 3):

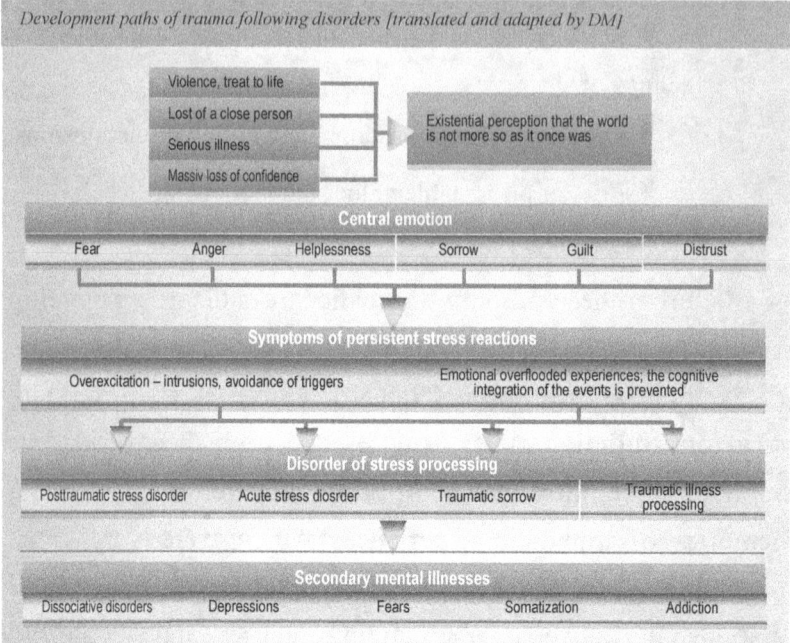

Figure 3: Development Pats of Trauma Following Disorders,
Source: (Michels Kliniken, 2008, p. 8)

Clinical psychology has analyzed and defined the issue of trauma very well. There are many therapeutic methods that deal with it. Nevertheless, in the last 14 years a new process occurred in which people are not only "curable", but also a positive attitude towards life will allow them to open up new horizons and improve their quality of life. This new approach within psychology is called »positive psychology«.

2.2. Positive Psychology

The term »positive psychology« seems, when generally applied in colloquial language, synonymous with general statements such as: "You should think positively, act positively." However, this term is not generally part of the concept of "Positive thinking"; it refers rather to a new type and a new area of psychology, which is relatively young as terminology in professional psychological and therapeutic areas.

> "Positive psychology is the self-designation of a research program established by the American psychologist Martin Seligman. There are normative positive items of Psychology treated such as happiness, optimism, security, trust, forgiveness and solidarity, which were little followed in the initial conflict- and problem-oriented psychology, according to Seligman." (Wikipedia, 2011)

Seligman is a senior professor of psychology at the University of Pennsylvania and the co-founder of a new direction – positive psychology. Its researches deal with the following topics:

> "Their representatives have presented interesting studies in the past few years, indicating how important a role positive emotions play, such as optimism, hope, gratitude and happiness for our mental health" (Fredrickson, 2011, p. 9).

2.2.1. Origin of Positive Psychology

Martin Seligman, as their new President in 1998, carried out official launch of positive psychology in the American Psychological Society (APA), according to its own sources. He made this decision together with the APA's predecessor, Ray Fowler and Mihaly Csikszentmihalyi on January 1st 1998 in Akumal, Mexico. The main reason for its creation was a deficiency in the development of clinical psychology (disease-related) in the following directions:

(1) human fulfillment and meaning of life and

2) support strengths (Pezent, 2011).

The emphasis of the established psychology has been on mental illnesses, negative sides and weaknesses of the people. Some psychologists and psychiatrists have earlier discovered and dealt with human basic needs and strengths. Some of them may be mentioned at this point:

> "Building on pioneering work by Rogers (1951), Maslow (1954, 1962), Jahoda (1958), Erikson (1963, 1982), Vaillant (1977), Deci and Ryan (1985), and Ryff and Singer (1996)—among many others – positive psychologists have enhanced our understanding of how, why, and under what conditions positive emotions, positive character, and the institutions that enable them flourish (e.g., Cameron, Dutton, & Quinn, 2003, Easterbrook, 2003, Gardner, Csikszentmihalyi, & Damon, 2001, Kahneman, Diener, & Schwarz, 1999, Murray, 2003, Vaillant, 2000)" (Seligman und Steen, 2005, p. 410).

The forerunner of positive psychology is actually humanistic psychology, in particular under Carl Rogers and Abraham Maslow as the leading authorities (Seligman, 2007). As older works are included especially by William James, John Dewey and G. Stanley Hall (Board dogs, 2001; Shaffer, 1978, cited in: Froh, 2004, p. 18).

Positive psychology is actually nothing new, it has only empirically examined previous ideas and questions about: what is worthy and valuable for human life and has summarized, deepened and finally made all that finally largely applicable (Seligman & Stehen, 2005). Their authors did not wish to replae clinical psychology, but have tried to complement it to create the balance between human distress or suffering and happiness (Seligman & Stehen, 2005).

One of three main pillars of positive psychology, the idea about the qualities or character virtues of individuals, is not a new subject. Seligman and his colleagues already have discovered it in Greek philosophy, especially in the teaching of Aristotle about virtues as character properties and guidelines for a happy life (Athanassoulis, 2004). Similar ideas about the character virtues are available also in Buddhism, Judaism and many other philosophies and religions (Seligman, 2007). Accordingly, the task of the positive psychology was not innovative. It has only combined and emphasized more the ancient doctrines of resource-oriented, positive forces in people and empirically researched it more thoroughly. Thanks to the strong financial support of the Rhoda Mayerson Foundation in 1999, the founders of positive psychology could very well manage to make a good start and begin to develop a good classification of the good character traits, strengths, and virtues that are necessary for the positive development of young people – "Values-In-Action", (Seligman, 2007). The John Templeton Foundation has also made a substantial financial contribution through various prizes for the best young positive psychologists (ibid.). Other financial supporters were the Annenberg and Pew foundations, Don Clifton and Jim Clifton, Father & Son, CEO of Gallup, etc. (ibid.). The financial effort was thus secured, to explore this idea empirically, to develop and also successfully spread the whole idea (Seligman, 2007).

2.2.2. Principles of Positive Psychology

Positive psychology is a general term for the research in three main areas:

(1) the study of positive emotions.

(2) the determination of positive character traits (strengths and virtues) and

(3) the examination and promotion of institutions that support the positive character traits (such as democracy, strong families, social institutions, etc.) and research which support the positive character properties (Seligman, 2007, xii). This third component is very important to keep in mind, to provide a wider support for clients in trauma therapy/counseling.

2.2.2.1 Positive Emotions

A strong and healthy person needs a solid foundation that can withstand difficulties of life. In positive psychology it is a positive basic attitude or basic setting (Fredrickson, 2011). It includes an understanding of a variety of interpersonal positive feelings: "appreciation, love, pleasure, deep sensed joy, hope, gratitude and much more" (Fredrickson, 2011, p. 18). Seligman emphases very often trust and hope (Seligman, 2007). These positive emotions have a positive long-term effect on the character and thereby affect the personality, interpersonal relationships and the whole environment (Fredrickson, 2011). It is noteworthy that positive emotions arise in everyday situations and moments, and they exercise a strong influence on the person's thinking and perception (Fredrickson, 2011). Life consists mainly of trifles and moments that satisfy the soul. If they are mastered in small steps, a general positive attitude can grow from day to day (Fredrickson, 2011). A positive atmosphere accomplishes not only the transforming of bad thoughts into good, but also the further expansion of the boundaries of the spirit to open up new possibilities (ibid.).

It is also possible to cope with unpleasant situations in a conciliatory and tolerant way: e.g. banal everyday situations like making a family game out of searching for lost shoes, in relationships with people and colleagues to build more confidence, etc. (Fredrickson, 2011). Although positive emotions remain brief, they play a major role in the long term and contribute to general well being (ibid.). They have a powerful influence on the mental level and activate all psychological resources (Fredrickson, 2011). In contrast, negative emotions and stress hormones block the resources of an individual and weaken the soul.

With positive feelings it is possible to deal with any situation and make the most of it (Fredrickson, 2011). This is actually the secret of resilience (ibid.). Feelings show the basic difference, how the general outcome, or mood will seem to be (ibid.). Positive feelings can be defined as »life-giving positivity« (ibid., p. 25); negative, however, as »potential of a hostile negativity« (Fredrickson, 2011, p. 25). Each person decides, with which of these approaches they should start every day. New opportunities arise with a positive attitude and consequently the soul and the body recover faster after setbacks; in relations with other people a stronger bond develops and even sleep is generally qualitatively better (ibid.).

The most beautiful moments and emotions that come from the heart do not last long (Fredrickson, 2011). Nevertheless, the research of Barbara L. Fredrickson, Professor of psychology at the University of North Carolina at Chapel Hill, United States, shows that the quantity of positive emotions is the crucial one – the so-called »positive quotient«, "[...] the measurable ratio between deep positive and heart-rending negative emotions" (Fredrickson, 2011, p. 30). Due to the studies, this ratio between positive and negative feelings is 3-to-1 (ibid.). If this ratio drops below the value, it creates a downward spiral of negativity, solidification and a sense of overstrain – a clear predictable attitude (ibid.). Conversely, the positive basic attitude leads to an upward spiral of positivity that leads to creativity, vitality and boost (Fredrickson, 2011, p. 30). Each person decides either for a positive, or for a negative course – to become a better person, more creative and more resistant, or to freeze in bad feelings and habits without them growing and developing further (Fredrickson, 2011). The positive quotient (3-to-1) makes the crucial difference (ibid.). This is also crucial in the case of trauma, a person decides then whether he/she wants to stay in a traumatic state, or will extricate him-/herself therefrom as quickly as possible.

To be happy and satisfied with life, something good should be done: to be engaged with the family, in society and at the workplace (Fredrickson, 2011). If life has a meaning, if somebody feels him-/herself as a key member of the society and seeks positive uplifting goals to do something valuable with his/her own life and to share good things with others, then a fulfilling life and a positive attitude towards life begin to happen (Fredrickson, 2011). The prerequisites for this are honesty and genuineness. Dishonestly positive statements and friendly play does more harm than good, because other people quickly realize whether someone is sincere or not (Fredrickson, 2011).

Happy and positive feelings indicate that everything is upright, that life is beautiful and successful, so that someone can feel safe and satisfied (Fredrickson, 2011). Fredrickson defines the following positive feelings, which themselves can manifest a positive attitude towards life: "[...] Joy, gratitude, enjoyment, interest, hope, pride, pleasure, inspiration, admiration and love" (Fredrickson, 2011, p. 57). There are also other positive forms, however, these mentioned are proven as the most widespread (Fredrickson, 2011). However, they are more than just a signal of health – based on the latest scientific research, they are also **the cause of health** (ibid.). They show that human emotional impulses and physical changes and reactions, particularly in dangers to life, act faster than the conscious thinking (ibid.). It is well known, that in any danger the pulse and the heart pounding are faster, blood circulation in extremities appears stronger and adrenal glands produce more cortisol, to consume more energy (ibid.). Also the glucose content increases in the bloodstream – escape impulse through fear – as a preparation of the body for the escape (ibid.). However, they restrict the human attention only to a danger (ibid.). Positive emotions, on the contrary, expand human horizons and awareness and increase the space of thinking and flexibility (Fredrickson, 2011). Joy makes us creative; interest moves us to explore and learn (ibid.). This means that positive emotions open the heart and the mind for responsiveness and creativity (Fredrickson, 2011). Attitudes arise from emotions: a negative, even neutral one inhibits our energy; a positive attitude, however, supports research, learning and growth, improving the quality of life (ibid.). Most recently, a positive attitude gives not only a better quality of life, but also the corresponding benefit – positive people live up to ten years longer (Fredrickson, 2011, p. 42).

The Type and intensity of feelings are rather more dependent on the **internal interpretation and adjustment**, then on external circumstances (ibid.). The same situation can in one individual product fear, but in no impact at all. Conversely, in an equally joyous situation someone can cheer and another can be totally untouched.

If the positive feelings are of very short duration and, moreover, compared with the negative ones, they disappear from memory relatively quickly, why are they so important to our health at all?

2.2.2.2 Physiology of Emotions

Feelings are the important basis and the main working field of trauma therapy. They show the actual psychological condition. How do they come into being and how can you consciously work with them as a therapist, or a pastor?

Although the human nerve system is not yet fully explored, neurobiology has discovered how our feelings function in physiological processes. The nerve cells communicate constantly with each other on an average 1000 contact points (Missler, 2003). This exchange of information is the basis of both health and disease (Missler, 2003). The great majority of neurons[7] perform the exchange of information in two ways:

(1) by **electrical** impulses along each nerve cell and

(2) by the **chemical** interactions between two neurons at synapses through messenger substances which are also called neurohormones.

This works so that the signal-sending nerve cell (the presynaptic neuron) first merge blisters or vesicles with its membrane – intracellular membrane vesicles, filled with messenger substances (Wikipedia, 2012) and then releases the freed content (messengers), or neuro-messengers (neurohormones), through briefly open sodium and potassium channels in the intracellular space (synaptic cleft between two touching nerve cells) (Wikipedia, 2012). The second neuron (or postsynaptic neuron – see the following sketch, Figure 4), receives the distributed messengers through the neuroreceptors or ion channels with receptor function (Wikipedia, 2012).

---

[7] Neurons with **chemical** synapses. There are also electrical synapses so-called »gap junctions«, where the tissue of two cells stands in contact, attached with »conexones« or »ion channels«. "In addition to the retina, this type of Synapse could be found quite often in the heart muscle between the muscle cells, in the smooth muscle in the cerebral cortex of rats" (Fischer, 2007).

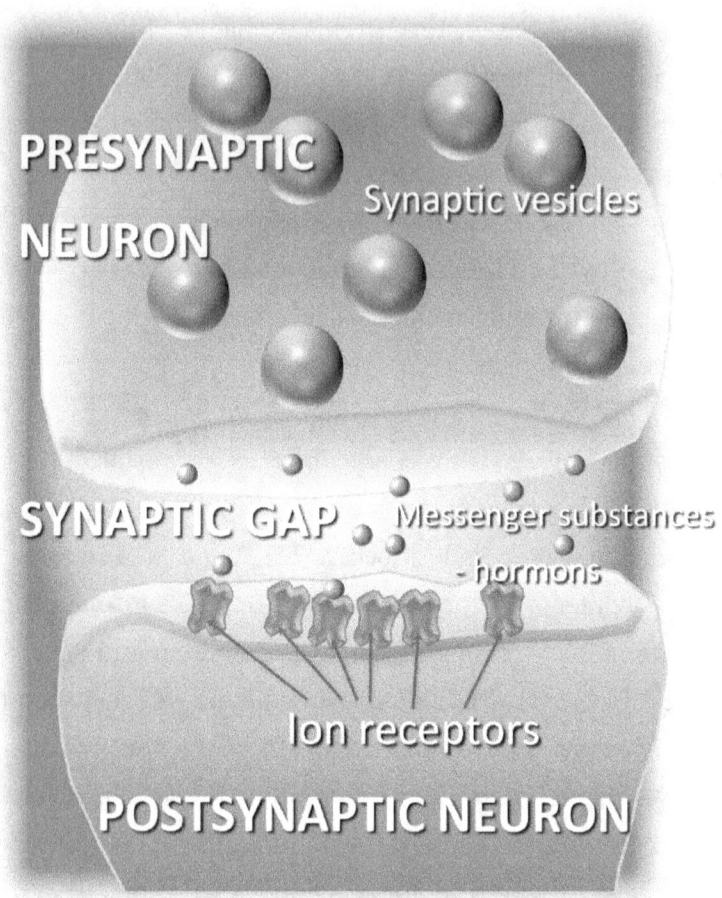

Figure 4: Synaptic Gap Between Two Neurons,
Source: graphic made by Dragan Mirkovic

This simply presented process happens between neurons in milliseconds. Nevertheless, there are two conditions for a successful communication between neurons: a well developed **neuroanatomical networking** (healthy grown, fully functional neurons, equipped together with enough messenger substance receptors) and also the necessary healthy physiology (sufficiently adapted amount of neurotransmitters). A deficiency of neurotransmitters serotonin and dopamine very often results as depression (Wikipedia, 2012). If however the body produces enough serotonin, but has not enough messenger substance receptors, for example, not enough serotonin receptors (as it is shown in a study from Bethesda, US State Maryland), this leads to the same result, even though the organism produces enough serotonin (Mediaprint infoverlag GmbH, 2004).

There are many different neurotransmitters in the human body. Some are produced in the nerve system, others, however, in various organs, especially in the endocrine glands. So-called »happiness hormones« are responsible for pleasant feelings. A proper knowledge of their functioning can be applied very well in (trauma) therapy cooperatively with the positive psychology:

Serotonin – "tissue-" or "fondle hormone". Its function is spread through the central nerve system, where it has an important role in the area of nerve pathway system, the cardiovascular system and the blood circle (Ohe, 2010). Its fourteen different serotonin receptors, distributed in various organs (brain, blood vessels, small intestine, blood platelets and lungs), control its various physiological functions (Ohe, 2010). Its deficiency can lead to both cardiovascular and digestive problems, as well to depression (Ohe, 2010; Wikipedia, 2010). Serotonin levels can be also increased through an intensification of positive feelings and experiences in the trauma therapy and a positive attitude towards life and, as a result, traumatic feelings can be overcome more easily.

Oxytocin – known as the "social hormone". His name means »quick birth« (Govi-Verlag, 2012). The first features, discovered in 1906, were the control of birth rate and secretion of breast milk by breastfeeding (Wikipedia, 2012). Besides its physiological, it has also a behavioral feature – the binding connection between mother and child and calming of the stress hormone cortisol by breastfeeding (Govi-Verlag, 2012). The latest research (research team headed by Markus Heinrich of the University of Zurich, ibid.) shows its effect in interpersonal relations – in the form of trust, loyalty and compassion (ibid.). Through petting the "social", "cuddle" and "love hormone" oxytocin is secreted in the pituitary gland hypothalamus. Today it is known through various studies in animals that this hormone, or neurotransmitter, is still responsible for positive social relationships (Pedersen & Prange, 1979; Pedersen, Ascher, Monroe, & Prange, 1982; Fahrenbach, Morrell & Pfaff, 1984; Winslow et al., 2000, cited in Wikipedia, 2012). It is therefore important to provide social support to stimulate this important hormone in trauma therapy by the patients.

Dopamine – joy hormone. On the one hand, the general role of dopamine is to increase activity and prevent depressive moods. On the other hand, its decreased production even causes depression and lack of drive (Mohr, 2010). It creates drive, serenity and vitality, well-being, powerful and harmonious movement and fine motor skills, enables good concentration and fast reactions, provides the courage and relieves fear, optimizes the heart function and circulation and activates the immune system (Mohr, 2010). Dopamine deficiency is very serious, because it can lead to severe depression (Mohr, 2010). However, an artificial addition is complicated due to the controlling blood-brain barrier. An artificial supply should be applied only in exceptional cases (in cardiovascular disorders and shock states – obviously only in intensive medicine care) (Mohr, 2010). It is very important to achieve the natural balance of dopamine through **positive activities** (that accomplish pleasure and enjoyment by patients) as in psychotherapy, as well as in everyday life.

Endorphins – hormones of happiness. Endorphins are chemically seen neuropeptides, named as opioid peptides α, β and γ group of the amino acid sequences; they are produces in the pituitary gland and the hypothalamus (Wikipedia, 2012) and resemble morphine, the strongest painkiller (ibid.). They control emotions such as pain and hunger, but stay also in connection with the production of sex hormones (ibid.). They are likewise responsible for the feeling of euphoria (Wikipedia, 2012) and also known as the hormones of happiness, because they cause pleasant feelings in positive and pleasant situations. Already by petting, endorphins associated with oxytocin are produced (Elviva.de, 2010). In successful sex (during orgasm) they spread through the whole body, similar to sports activities and efforts, as a "reward" for the effort (Elviva.de, 2010).

The latest research on the University of Michigan showed that endorphins are actually responsible for the placebo effect. If a patient is of good faith, then a (placebo) drug will help and endorphins are produced and the pain is reduced on the natural basis (Lehnen-Beyel, 2005). That's one more reason to strengthen the aspect of faith in therapy and pastoral care, to put the inner resources in response mode against the trauma.

Noradrenaline or norepinephrine (INN). This is a neurotransmitter and a hormone which is produced in the adrenal medulla and the locus coeruleus (Wikipedia, 2012). It is related to adrenaline and stimulates the cardiovascular system. In the clinical picture of heart failure, a pathologically increased concentration of norepinephrine in the blood has been found (Wikipedia, 2012). Its most important role as a neurotransmitter was portrayed in the central nervous system and the sympathetic nervous system similar to adrenaline (ibid.).

As a hormone, it is emitted from the adrenal glands in the blood as an escape reflex, to regulate the blood pressure (ibid.). Norepinephrine is used in intensive medicine care as an emergency medication to successfully treat various shock states: septic, cardiogenic, and anaphylactic shock, as well as poisoning with vasodilation and hypotension (Wikipedia, 2012). Of course, there are also contra-indications, which are known to medicine. Noradrenaline energizes, enables, makes us awake and responsive and makes us attentive, motivated and committed. Noradrenaline often occurs in connection with the serotonin and dopamine. It is obviously necessary to support the patients in a positive manner (for e.g. with pleasant activities) to allow enough of this hormone to be produced.

Phenethylamine (PEA), chemical name: 2-phenyl-ethylamine. A precursor of benzylisoquinoline alkaloids is found mainly in the brain and urinary, but even exists in the plant world – in bitter almond oil and cocoa beans (so also in the chocolate) (Wikipedia, 2012). As root substance of catecholamine and many hallucinogens, it is responsible for the romantic love symptoms: wet hands, "a lump in my throat" and "butterflies in the stomach" (Wikipedia, 2012).

In larger concentrations, phenethylamine can function acidly on the skin and mucous membranes, in low concentrations. However, it causes:

> "[...] physical alertness, feeling of increased vigor, strength, confidence, speech urge, impairment of the judgment, nervousness, restlessness of movement" (IFA-Institut für Arbeitsschutz der Deutschen Gesetzlichen Unfall-versicherungen, 2005).

Summarized, positive feelings contribute not only to a good mood, but have the main function of the physiological communication in our nerve system. They create healthy physiological processes, while negative (stress) feelings or hormones, long-term without relaxation, block a healthy neurological connection and hence also affect health.

"Prolonged stress can lead to hormonal disorders and also be a risk factor for depressive illness" (Kroll, 2012). In normal situations stress hormones (substance messenger) adrenaline and noradrenaline are involved. However, persistent and chronic stress "[...] changes psychosomatic reaction patterns and other stress hormones, such as cortisol, are produced" (Medmonitor GmbH & Co. KG, 2008).

From all of the above reasons, it is very important in trauma therapy to develop these techniques, as well as in counseling and pastoral care, not only during the therapy sessions, but also in everyday life. Positive emotions should be regularly produced by appropriate activities, to reduce negative stress hormones and promote healthy relaxation. Although after a trauma a negative mood prevails, it is necessarily important to find out with the patient what are the appropriate activities for them, that cause positive mood and emotions in them (e.g. music, reading, friendship circle, contact with nature, etc. – everything that fits the best to the person concerned), as part of the therapy / counseling process.

2.2.2.3 Positive Character Traits

Positive psychology is not only about the positive feelings and activities that promote happiness, but also character properties that allow healthy lifestyle characteristics, not only in good, but also in very serious situations and stages of life. Character strengths and virtues are – courage, perspective, integrity, fairness, loyalty, etc. (Seligman, 2007). Negative traits and emotions (personality disorders, psychoses and neuroses) can be prevented through positive ones and be replaced by optimism, hope, social skills and courage (Seligman, 2007).

Positive psychology has developed six main features / virtues and 24 corresponding strengths in the expanse of character with their definitions (see the following table).

Table 1
Classification of 6 Virtues and 24 Character Strengths (Peterson & Seligman, 2004)

Virtue and strength	Definition
1. Wisdom and knowledge	Cognitive strengths that entail the acquisition and use of knowledge
Creativity	Thinking of novel and productive ways to do things
Curiosity	Taking an interest in all of ongoing experience
Open-mindedness	Thinking things through and examining them from all sides
Love of learning	Mastering new skills, topics, and bodies of knowledge
Perspective	Being able to provide wise counsel to others
2. Courage	Emotional strengths that involve the exercise of will to accomplish goals in the face of opposition, external or internal
Authenticity	Speaking the truth and presenting oneself in a genuine way
Bravery	*Not* shrinking from threat, challenge, difficulty, or pain
Persistence	Finishing what one starts
Zest	Approaching life with excitement and energy
3. Humanity	Interpersonal strengths that involve "tending and befriending" others
Kindness	Doing favors and good deeds for others
Love	Valuing close relations with others
Social intelligence	Being aware of the motives and feelings of self and others
4. Justice	Civic strengths that underlie healthy community life
Fairness	Treating all people the same according to notions of fairness and justice
Leadership	Organizing group activities and seeing that they happen
Teamwork	Working well as member of a group or team
5. Temperance	Strengths that protect against excess
Forgiveness	Forgiving those who have done wrong
Modesty	Letting one's accomplishments speak for themselves
Prudence	Being careful about one's choices; *not* saying or doing things that might later be regretted
Self-regulation	Regulating what one feels and does
6. Transcendence	Strengths that forge connections to the larger universe and provide meaning
Appreciation of beauty and excellence	Noticing and appreciating beauty, excellence, and/or skilled performance in all domains of life
Gratitude	Being aware of and thankful for the good things that happen
Hope	Expecting the best and working to achieve it
Humor	Liking to laugh and tease; bringing smiles to other people
Religiousness	Having coherent beliefs about the higher purpose and meaning of life

Figure 5: Classification of the 6 virtues and 24 strengths,
Source: Peterson & Seligman, 2004, cited in:
Seligman & Steen, 2005, p. 410

Thus it is clear that for a healthy and happy personality external conditions are not primarily responsible, but moreover inner positive character traits and attitudes toward life and the fellows (Seligman, 2007). Though the personality structure, past experiences and education are very difficult to change, positive psychology suggests that humans have the ability to learn new skills and consequently to be changed positively and constructively (Seligman, 2007). It is possible to achieve a new perspective, new patterns of thought and behavior (Seligman, 2007) and thus to restructure one's whole life.

In positive psychology, there are two types of personality strengths:

1) **character virtues** with ethical values and

2) **talents** with no ethical values (Seligman, 2007).

The first group requires the strength of will, the second one not necessarily so (ibid.). In positive psychology character traits can be learned but talents, in contrast, which are relatively automatic, not always so (ibid.). That's why the concept of faith and personal responsibility is central for the development of character and thus also for positive psychology (Seligman, 2007). The personal activity of will of the patient is necessarily important in the treatment process of positive psychology, in contrast to the therapeutic psychology, where more the process of "molding" or "manipulation" of passive patients takes place (Seligman, 2007).

2.2.2.4 Institutions that Support the Positive Character Traits

According to positive psychology, the cultural and social institutions also play an important role, as e.g. board of trustees, various clubs and social organizations for children and young people, cultural and religious rituals, etc., that support positive character values and develop: leadership skills, ability to work, responsibility, duty, loyalty and all other virtues and strengths (Seligman, 2007). One of the most important institutions that support children and young people is marriage, or family (Seligman, 2007). Children and adolescents with both biological parents, for example, have much less mental disorders and in contrast more success in their training (Seligman, 2007). They are able to develop more stable relationships in the life and so a higher social intelligence (ibid.). It has mainly to do with the development of the binding ability of the children. Through various studies of the binding theory by scientists, it is found that the relationship between the caregiver and the child in early childhood is very crucial (Wikipedia, 2007).

It is important that clients get good support from the relevant institutions (including from the family and relatives), not only to recover more quickly from the trauma, but also to permanently strengthen their own personality. Accordingly, it is important to find this systemic support and promote it in psychotherapy, counseling and pastoral care.

Thus a good connection develops between the "environmental awareness" ('environment') in the clinical psychology (ibid.), which includes external influences on the individuals and the personality strengths, which are very often missed in clinical psychology. In this respect positive psychology is very similar to the systemic psychotherapy that is also greatly concerned with the family and the whole support system of a person.

2.2.3. Factors and Definition of Happiness

In positive psychology »happiness«, »positive attitude« and »positive emotions« are emphasized as objectives of positive psychology (Seligman, 2007, Fredrickson 2011). Seligman called it: »authentic happiness« (Seligman, 2007), that depends on inner fundamental strengths and is practiced in everyday life and is not dependent only on external delights, attractiveness or wealth (Seligman, 2007). So character virtues, life meaning and integrity form the solid foundation of a healthy personality and serve as a protection against disaster and mental disorders (ibid.). Seligman believes that all these are the keys of resilience (ibid.). Therefore, **the main task of trauma therapy is to identify personal strengths and virtues** (ibid.). True happiness is accordingly not a temporary feeling, but a process of construction of an inner positive attitude and life change. Therefore the effects of the therapy / counseling are visible not only during the therapy process, but also long after.

2.2.4. Factors of Life Satisfaction

Despite the general belief that prosperity provides happiness, the reality is different. With the improvement of living conditions, emotional disorders and diseases have correspondingly increased in the society (both in Europe and in America) – suicide, addictions, etc. (Lukas, 2011).

According to positive psychology, the factors of life satisfaction lie not necessarily in external circumstances, but in the inner attitude to life and in the person's character (Seligman, 2007). The main factor of a virtuous character and thus also of happiness is **philanthropy** (Seligman, 2007). It gives to life not only a higher meaning, but reinforces the inner strengths and improves the psychic abilities as a kind of reward – much more than simple pleasure and delights (Seligman, 2007). The expression of philanthropy is kindness, a kind of self-denial (Seligman, 2007). Consequently, positive character strengths and virtues bring positive emotions as a reward for themselves (ibid.). Negative character traits, however, bring negative feelings with themselves and thus also mental and physical disorders and diseases (ibid.). In this area, the results of research in the positive psychology is a confirmation of Christian love, which is the highest law of life:

> Matthew 22,39And a second like *unto it* is this, Thou shalt love thy neighbor as thyself (American Standard Version).

2.3. Comparison Between Positive and Clinical Psychology

According to Seligman much in psychology and psychiatry is discovered about how and why various disorders and diseases arise and grow, but less about how patients can constructively and actively be healed from them and how they can grow and be stronger (Seligman, 2004). Psychologists, psychiatrists and counselors were mainly the experts who should make the final decisions for the patient (ibid.). They have the knowledge (know-how) and they have in their hands the fate of their clients. According to Seligman, patients and advice seekers are more passive objects of therapy and not active subjects who can change somewhat freely and independently (Seligman, 2004). Thus the responsibility wasn't on the clients (ibid.). They learned to be dependent on therapists for many years and had to learn only shortly before the end of the therapy how to separate themselves from them. Independence is thus not properly developed.

The second main problem in psychology was the lack of interest for the positive – for the ingenious, to develop personal talents (Seligman, 2004). Clinical psychology and psychotherapy focused mainly on psychological problems and diseases, and not on the personal strengths.

The third problem of the clinical psychology was the lack of positive interventions, to develop the happiness of clients (ibid.).

This concept of disease healing, or »illness ideology« (Joseph & Linley, 2008), has brought relatively little long-term improvement in society (ibid.). The number of patients and mental illnesses has grown, but not the efficiency of the therapeutic approaches. Seligman has noted that the trend / development of the positive quality of therapy is missing (Seligman, 2004). The clinical psychology has developed a medical language of psychopathology, with the emphasis on the human weaknesses and diseases, but not on their strengths and the mental health (Joseph & Linley, 2008). In the area of war trauma the emphasis is on the disorder (in the context of the war trauma it is the post traumatic stress disorder - PTSD) and not on posttraumatic growth (ibid.).

As the new President of the APA, Seligman has together with the well-known leading psychologists Mihály Csíkszentmihályi, the author of the concept of "flow" (Wikipedia, 2012) and Raymond D. Fowler, the former President of the "American Psychological Association" (APA) (Wikipedia, 2011) developed a new concept, dealing first with the resources of the people and not with their weaknesses and slights. The old schools of Psychology have developed methods and classifications how to measure and organize personality disorders and mental diseases. In contrast to that, positive psychology has developed a classification of strengths and characteristics using diagnostic and measurement methods (Seligman, 2004). Furthermore, positive psychology has also discovered the relationship of the activities between the two hemispheres of the brain that cause happiness (Seligman, 2004).

Usually, the rest of psychology deals mainly with sick people; positive psychology, however, with healthy and happy people, searching for the reasons why they differ from others less fortunate than themselves (ibid.).

Additionally, positive psychology criticizes clinical psychology that the basis of the main assumptions of the highly educated intellectual spirits from 19th-century America is missed, namely:

- „[…] that there is a human „nature"
- That action proceeds from character
- That character comes in two forms, both equally fundamental – bad character, and good or virtuous („angelic") character" (Seligman, 2007, p. 123).

How did it happen that clinical psychology has neglected the concept of character and personal responsibility so much?

2.3.1. Reasons why Psychology has Neglected the Idea of Character in a Large Scale

According to Seligman, the character, as a psychological concept (up to the 19th century as the basis of psychology), has almost completely disappeared in the 20th century (Seligman, 2007). Why and how?

After the civil war in the 19th century in the United States many riots, strikes and violence took place in the country due to high unemployment (ibid.). Through various changes in the society bad character traits and therefore negative patterns of behavior have become dominant (ibid.). Living in the 20th century has become much harder and has negatively affected many people – poverty, overload at work, poor and cramped living conditions, very poor education and at the same time the moral decay of the whole society (Seligman, 2007). The old ethical explanation that bad deeds arise out of a bad character could no longer explain the common reality (ibid.). It was noted that the majority of these dissatisfied people has lived in very bad living conditions without any training and in very bad health condition (ibid.). To be able to correctly interpret and explain everything, a new teaching – social science - came into being, which declares that not people, but the circumstances are responsible for their behavior. The greatest exponents of this new idea were Freud, Marx, Darwin and others (ibid.). Personal responsibility and their own character have been getting stronger dependent on society and the whole system (ibid.). According to Seligman, people have developed the "learned helplessness" as a main approach to life (Seligman 1999), which has led to a general depression in many persons. The foundation of this new doctrine is evolution, according to which the survival of an organism, or a living species, finally depends of the principle of adaptability to external living conditions. Conversely, the life circumstances (climate, environmental and living conditions) determine the survivability of a species.

This resulted in a new understanding of social and living conditions, and thus a new scientific discipline – social science (Seligman, 2007). The bad behavior could be explained now by poor living conditions and thus be justified (Seligman, 2007). According to Seligman, social science has left the old "character model", so that character played no more a role in the new American psychology of behavior (ibid.). A new social concept emerged – egalitarianism, where all people are equally can be considered and treated (ibid.). It is no longer the responsibility of the individual in the psychological and ethical, but only in the judicial field. People are considered by law to be responsible citizens, but they are not psychologically trained for that. That's why the whole social system has double standards (ibid.). Positive psychologists see their mission to lead society and individuals to a responsible and constructive attitude and approach (Seligman, 2007).

According to Seligman, although psychology has ignored the concept of character, its importance in real life has not become less (ibid.). He explained his meaning as follows:

> „Good and bad character remained firmly entrenched in our laws, our politics, the way we raised our children, and the way we talked and thought about why people do what they do. Any science that does not use character as a basic idea (or at least explain character and choice away successfully) will never be accepted as a useful account of human action" (Seligman, 2007, p. 126).

Furthermore, the only discipline of psychology, which dealt with the character in the 20th century, was the study of personality under Gordon Allport as its founder, who has stressed the virtues of character and the importance of the personality structure (Seligman, 2007). One another expert, today one of the leading specialists in the topic of personality, is Christopher Peterson (ibid.). The advocates of positive psychology claim that it is extremely important to emphasize the importance of character or personality (Seligman, 2007). Since the term "character" is more normative – as American Protestants of the 19th century have understood it – positive psychology defines character properties descriptively as »personality« and means whereby virtues, which are generally recognized in all cultures and nations as positive values (Seligman, 2007).

On the one hand, the concept of character is not so strongly represented in clinical psychology as in positive psychology. On the other hand, there are similarities between positive psychology and other philosophical and psychotherapeutic approaches.

2.3.2. Positive Psychology and Other Philosophical and Psychotherapeutic Approaches

Positive psychology is not an invention of recent decades. Its first philosophical basis was the idea of the Greek philosopher Aristotle about the six virtues of human character:

- "Wisdom and knowledge
- Courage
- Love and humanity

- Justice
- Temperance
- Spirituality and transcendence"(Seligman, 2007, p. 9).

The experts in positive psychology have found these six virtues in each of all two hundred other sources – some of them are Plato, Aquinas and Augustine, in the Old Testament and Talmud, Confucius, Buddha, Lao-Tze, Bushido (Samurai code), in the Koran, in the words of Benjamin Franklin, Upanishads and others (ibid.). That is why these noble character traits have emerged as something common in nearly all religions and philosophical traditions (ibid.). That has brought Seligman from the disease model of clinical psychology toward using the strength model of the character, much like the ancient philosophers have dealt with the qualities and strengths of the human nature (Seligman, 2007). This idea of the positive forces and resources of humans are also included in earlier psychological works (see Chapter 2.2.1).

Seligman sees positive psychology as a summary of all resource-oriented works and psychological approaches. It is not itself a breakthrough in this area. Even before the emergence of positive psychology, various authors have dealt with the positive and healthy forces in human beings. The basics were already set. The main contribution of positive psychology is in the all-encompassing empirical research in the field of positive emotions, character traits, favorable conditions and the institutional structures that promote happiness (Seligman & Steen, 2005). Therefore, there are many similarities with other resource-oriented approaches in psychology, psychotherapy and counseling, such as by Carl Rogers and Antonowsky with their research on resilience (Reddemann, 2011, p. 42).

Although common psychology doesn't deal so much with the term "character" in its different approaches, character virtues from positive psychology are comparable with other values of the human psyche, which are measurable with other psychological methods:

> "For example, the virtue of humanity can be achieved by kindness, philanthropy, the capacity to love and be loved, sacrifice, or compassion. The virtue of temperance can be exhibited by modesty and humility, disciplined self-control, or prudence and caution" (Seligman, 2007, p. 131).

Although positive psychology has caused a drastic turnaround from the negative to the positive in the world of psychology in America, such a development in the German-speaking world originated in the 90th – under the name of »resource orientation« or »promotion of development« by Fürstenau, further developed by Grawe (Reddemann, 2011, p. 44). Furthermore, Milton Erickson's school and the systemic therapy have devoted themselves to this area (ibid.). Accordingly, it can be conclusive that the basics (resource orientation) of positive psychology already exist in German psychology for last few decades.

2.3.3. Goal of Positive Psychology in Comparison with the Common Objective of the Counseling

The goal of positive psychology can be well summarized by the following statement:

> "The field of positive psychology at the subjective level is about valued subjective experiences: well-being, contentment, and satisfaction (in the past); hope and optimism (for the future); and flow and happiness (in the present). At the individual level, it is about positive individual traits: the capacity for love and vocation, courage, interpersonal skill, aesthetic sensibility, perseverance, forgiveness, originality, future mindedness, spirituality, high talent, and wisdom. At the group level, it is about the civic virtues and the institutions that move individuals toward better citizenship: responsibility, nurturance, altruism, civility, moderation, tolerance, and work ethic." (Seligman & Csíkszentmihályi 2000, p. 5)

Although all these goals are the secondary constituent of all counseling and psychotherapy approaches, they are in positive psychology the priority – especially the resource strength of an individual. Hereby can also the developments that affect not only the clients but also be added the social and political structures. Positive psychology is not a substitute for other psychological and psychotherapeutic approaches, but a complement of psychological research both on human suffering, weaknesses and problems, as well as on the sources of joy, strength and overcoming of mental disorders (Seligman & Steen, 2005).

According to Seligman, the main difference is in handling and the kind of therapy. In clinical psychology a patient, or advice seeker is more a passive object and the therapist, in contrast, active in the area of curative "design" or so-called "manipulation" (Seligman, 2007). The patient must trust the psychotherapist, obey and follow him/her (ibid.). In positive psychology, however, the patient must be more active – even to make their own decisions, to discover new paths, to create and appropriate the strengths and virtues applicable in everyday life (Seligman, 2007). It requires much more the power of faith, a process of learning and an active change (ibid.). This claim of Seligman can be true for clinical types of psychotherapy based on psychoanalysis, but not for resource-oriented psychotherapy approaches that exist here in Germany and Europe.

Seligman defines the main difference between other clinical psychological approaches and positive psychology together with the emphasis, also in the goal setting. Clinical psychology tries to bring a person back to a normal state ("to heal"), where positive psychology emphasizes personal strengths and virtues of sufferance, not only to heal, but also to help them actively how to be permanently happier and more successful (Seligman, 2007). In this process, it is important not to find a general solution to prescribe to all patients, because everyone is different, but to encourage a patient, to ask: "what tells you your inner self, your inner wisdom, your inner physician" (Reddemann, 2011, p. 47). Deep inner needs are actually relevant to how patients can be helped.

2.3.3.1 General Differences and Similarities Between Psychology and Pastoral Care

In the following aspect, pastoral care differs from psychology: for the common psychology approaches, as well as for positive psychology, a patient is the source of the solution. In pastoral ministry, God is this source of fulfillment of human needs. But this necessarily does not apply to all pastoral approaches, especially not to those that work almost purely with deep psychoanalysis.[8] The task of Christian therapists / ministers, after a diagnostic procedure, is to help the patients, with regard to the search for solutions, to strengthen their confidence and faith in God and to bring their basic attitude in line with him, so that God can heal the person through his divine positive values. This moment is missing in psychology, although some psychological studies have found that positive faith certainly promotes the whole health (see the chapter: "Research on the influence of faith on health"). Pastoral care is not only just about the psyche (»soul«), such as in psychology, but about the whole person, as stated in the following text:

> 1 Thess. 5,22 „Abstain from every form of evil. 23 Now may the God of peace himself sanctify you completely, and may your **whole spirit and soul and body** be kept blameless at the coming of our Lord Jesus Christ. 24 He

---

[8] In Germany there are also, within the pastoral approaches, particularly in circles of the Evangelic State Church, deep psychoanalytical concepts (especially from Freud and Jung), such as Otto Pfister and Joachim Scharfenberg, that are offered to all pastors as a part of the theological studies named "Clinical Pastoral Education" („Klinische Seelsorge-Ausbildung" - KSA) (Dietrich, 2012).

who calls you is faithful; he will surely do it" (English Standard Version) [**bold** – DM].[9]

It's about a positive attitude to life what **includes the whole person and the whole life**. This is not only a symptom treatment, but also an establishing of an emotional / mental, as well as the physical immune system. In this moment is pastoral care similar to positive psychology, which deals not only with symptoms, but also much more with general »psychological immune system«.

However, the common element in pastoral care and psychology is that human mental / emotional needs should be fulfilled. The goal is similar, only the solutions are somewhat different. That is why it is good to combine these different approaches to complement each other, especially in areas where they are compatible with each other. In spite of some big differences in some directions, such as psychoanalysis and positive psychology, the first can be a good diagnosis, the other a good solution. You can also involve behavioral therapy, to get the result quickly, if it is urgent. Nevertheless, it is advisable to develop a combined approach to various aspects of both the diagnosis and the creation of a successful therapy. Today the Christian pastoral care also goes more and more in the direction of psychotherapy, although something differ – some of them go more in the direction of pure spirituality[10], the other schools however in the direction of

---

[9] Cited from the Website: http://biblia.com/books/esv/1Th5.12 on April 14th 2014.

[10] E.g.: E. Thurneysen, J. Adams und J. & P. Sandford (Dietrich, 2012)

psychoanalysis of Freud and Jung[11]. A balance is recommended to selectively combine two components.

2.3.4. Perspective of Positive Psychology on Post-traumatic Stress

Unlike in the clinical (disease) model, which deals mainly with post traumatic disorder, positive psychology emphasizes resilience and post-traumatic growth, which can be found as an idea in many historical and philosophical sources throughout human history: personal benefit can be developed through suffering (Jaffe, 1985, Yalom & Lieberman, 1991, cited in Joseph & Linley, 2008).[12] Although the approaches of post-traumatic stress and post-traumatic growth were developed independently, positive psychology is trying to combine and to integrate both approaches – thereby to achieve both: to deal with suffering and trauma, but also to constructively build strengths and virtues to overcome the trauma (Joseph & Linley, 2008).

An integration of these two models –clinical and positive psychology – is therefore recommended, because you can use both two dimensions, a good diagnostic (clinical) model, as well as a solution-oriented approach. Such a model should be integrated in the next step with Christian pastoral care and Christian psychology. Thus, all dimensions of

---

[11] E.g.: O. Pfister, J. Scharfenberg und W. Jentsch (Dietrich, 2012).

[12] A similar idea can be found in Buddhism and Christianity, but also in the European literature (Dante Alighieri, Fyodor Dostoevsky, Kierkegaard and Nietzsche) (Joseph & Linley, 2008).

psychological-pastoral support would be used. This is my recommendation for further research and development. Such a model, that goes in that direction, already exists here in Germany under the name of »biblical therapeutic counseling«, founded by Michael Dietrich,[13] that is referred to as »holistic pastoral care« (Dietrich, 2012).

2.3.5. Approach of Positive Psychology in Counseling in Germany

Although positive psychology has arrived officially in the professional psychological circles since 1999, it has still not reached German and European psychological work area so well as in the United States. One of the best-known experts in trauma therapy in Germany, Luise Reddemann says about it:

> "In the English-speaking countries the ideas of the positive psychology have encountered broad interest. This is according to my knowledge, less the case in Germany" (Reddemann, 2011, p. 42).

Partly because much time is necessary to establish that from American practice in the German one. The first book of "Positive psychology" by Ann E. Auhagen about research approaches of German-speaking researchers in the above-mentioned area appeared only in 2004 (Reddemann, 2011). On the other hand, positive psychology is nothing new in Europe, especially in Germany, because the resilience-research was available since 1990s. For a detailed description of what is positive psychology, Reddemann recommends a balance of

---

[13] Webseite: http://www.bts-ips.de.

psycho-traumatology and positive psychology, or "Health ideology" (Reddemann, 2011, p. 45).

The main contribution of positive psychology to traumatology is, on the one hand, in prevention – how to prevent various mental disorders and wide-ranging diseases systemically (which is still in a process of development). It emphases the personal strengths as the best protection against mental disorders and diseases. On the other hand, it works also with different weaknesses, but indirectly – not especially to heal mental diseases and disorders directly, but to develop personal strengths that have the beneficial effect of a barrier against the mental disorders and diseases (Lopez & Snyder, 2011).

Luise Reddemann summarizes the contribution of positive psychology to trauma therapy as follows:

> "It remains however to be the merit of positive psychology in the present time on the need to rely on scientific interest in the healthy mental areas. Therefore, I recommend reading by authors like Auhagen, Seligman and especially Linley & Joseph (2011)" (Reddemann, 2011, p. 51).

2.4. Trauma Therapy

Although the request for trauma therapy comes mainly from patients, it is important for all therapists, counselors or ministers to identify when the therapy/counseling is absolutely necessary. Traumatic experiences and their consequences are actually only a functional coping mechanism of personal or group management strategy and therefore not necessarily a need for therapy (Lanfranchi, 2004). Each person or family has his or her own coping and resilience methods (ibid.). The ratified indications are therapy or counseling for not traumatic experiences themselves, but serious difficulties in living with them (Lanfranchi, 2004). In addition, it should be taken into consideration in therapy / counseling, that permission status uncertainty and no perspective of life in many cases can be a psychological burden for immigrants (ibid.). On the one hand, »victim identity« can already arise thereby, on the other hand rigid enemy images can be constructed, which can involve also teachers and therapists, especially if the question in counseling / therapy may be considered on suspicious and painstaking manner (Lanfranchi, 2004). Caution and understanding are necessary here.

Trauma therapy is a general term that includes various application modes, depending on the psychological approach. Any school of psychology or psychotherapy has its own methodology and goal setting in therapy. A well-known method is e.g. "trauma-centered psychotherapy", where the therapy process deals primarily with the trauma. It involves four phases:

1. **Case history** (with the diagnosis);
2. **Stabilization work / resource work**;
3. **Trauma exposure / trauma synthesis**, and
4. **Integration** (Passow, 2005).

The renowned author on the subject of trauma, Luise Reddemann, recommended PITT – psychodynamic imaginative trauma therapy (Reddemann, 2011).

Wampold et al. (2010) have made a helpful list of trauma therapy factors and steps, which are important for a successful treatment of post-traumatic disorder:

- "Convincing psychological explanations that are acceptable to the patients
- Development and promotion of a safe, respectful and trustworthy therapeutic relationship
- Mutually developed agreements on the tasks and goals of therapy
- Promoting hope and establishing a sense of self-efficacy
- Psycho-education about post-traumatic disorders
- Possibility to speak about the traumatic experiences
- Concern for the safety of the patient, particularly in the case of victimization, as it happens in domestic violence, neighborhood violence and abuse
- Offers of help, how patients can learn to prevent re-victimization
- Identifying of the resources of patients, their strengths, life surviving skills, as well as of intra- and interpersonal resources and of resilience construction
- Learning of coping mechanisms
- Exposure
- Learning of meaning of the traumatic experiences and of the reactions of the patients to the event
- Encouraging acknowledgments of patients to ascribe changes to themselves
- Encouragement, to bring about social support and use
- Prevention of relapse" (Reddemann, 2011, p. 27).

After traumatic incidents and losses, people need some time to process grief and depression. Only so they can express themselves in the therapy or counseling, where it is best for therapist/counselor to see their pain not different than they self (Lopez & Snyder, 2011). To understand them better, you need detailed information about their experiences with the help of detailed questions. The survey questions can look like this:

"Necessary" questions for a biography

The story about the war experience is usually very difficult for war-traumatized people. Nevertheless, it is important to collect the necessary data to diagnose the problem and therefore to find the necessary solutions for therapy, counseling or pastoral care. The following points can help to make a suitable questionnaire:

- Date of birth (war time, pre- or post-war time)
- Place of birth (bombed city? Former German eastern territories?)
- Residence during the war and the post-war period
- Important events and experiences
- Function or status of the father in the war (followers, perpetrators, victims?), prisoner of war, war injuries
- Social situation and living conditions of the family at the end of the war
- Fate of family members
- Drawing of escape routes
- Family photos
- Time witnesses reports.

It is of enormous importance to show understanding for traumatized people; the encouragement to create a new perspective on life is even more important.

2.4.1. War-Trauma therapy

In the process of trauma therapy or counseling, it is recommended at the beginning of the treatment to inform patients what is war-trauma and how our nerve system and body respond to and finally – how to deal with it. It is very helpful to develop the therapy or counseling in such a manner, that patients feel comfortable and safe (Reddemann, 2011). If they do not want to talk about their trauma, because it is too troublesome for them, one should not exert pressure on them to avoid re-trauma (Reddemann, 2011). Furthermore, it is important to explain to them why they behave as they do and that it is typical for such an experience (ibid.). To develop a self-understanding is also even better for control and stress-reduction (ibid.). Thus it creates self-affirmation and self-appreciation, which is very important to traumatized patients (ibid.), which are very often loaded with a sense of guilt (Zahlner, 2008). The same applies to the affirmation and appreciation of symptoms (Reddemann, 2011). Although the traumatic events are extremely unpleasant – a good way to cure them is "to deal with them and to integrate them, even if this trying itself may be proved to be destructive later in life" (Reddemann, 2011, p. 26).

2.4.1.1 War Trauma Therapy with Positive Psychology

Trauma-centered models have developed many methods of war trauma therapy. The scope of this study is not wide enough to mention all of them in detail. It involves in particular positive psychology. Its main contribution, in relation to war trauma therapy, is a positive approach to the issue and to emphasize the personal resources and the use of potential after the traumatic events. Elements of this positive post-traumatic development can be summarized as follows:

1. Joseph and Linley emphasize especially the work on **images** that must be processed in trauma therapy (Reddemann, 2011).

2. Tedeschi and Calhoun have made a particularly large contribution to the concept of »**traumatic growth**« (Reddemann, 2011) [see the chapter "Post-traumatic growth"]. This means that in war trauma therapy it is very important to ask about the positive changes "that go in the direction of more mental maturity and which were clearly triggered by traumatic experiences" (Reddemann, 2011, p. 47f). All consultants should be prepared to listen to the patients about their suffering and trauma (ibid.), to show their own willingness to understand. A further step is recognition of the positive moments that have arisen from it.

3. Linley (2003) emphasizes **wisdom** as a process and as a result of the adaptation to the trauma (Reddemann, 2011). Baltes has developed a similar concept of wisdom as:

> "[...] rich factual knowledge as well as rich procedural knowledge about the facts of life. The knowledge of life contexts, exemplary education, family and work. Compared to different works and views in belief. **Recognizing and dealing with the uncertainties of life**. [Highlighting L.R.]" (Reddemann, 2011, p. 48).

To this concept belongs also the ability to learn from one's own mistakes or those of others (ibid.). The concept of post-traumatic wisdom as a successful adaptation to traumatic experience has three components:

1. A wise individual realizes that the life in this world is uncertain and learns to deal with this uncertainty accordingly (Reddemann, 2011, S. 48f). Such people are open to life changes (ibid.).

2. Wise people integrate their emotions and cognition successfully, they understand their own emotions, but are also able to control them intelligently (ibid.).

3. Wise people accept the limitation in life and thereby the boundaries of human life itself – namely death (Reddemann, 2011). On the other hand, they appreciate the value of life with its fragility and its limits (ibid.). Thus, they learn also to think beyond themselves – to create transcendence – to be involved with others (Reddemann, 2011). For this purpose the higher meaning of life and the belief in a reality greater than man is also very helpful. This can be e.g. faith in God and eternal life and that all injustices will someday be eliminated. It can also be followed by understanding of the most difficult question about the origin of evil, from the Biblical point of view,[14] what helps to patients to understand, why they have undergone such experiences. Understanding sinful human nature may well help the patients to classify the experience easier. More will be said about it at the end of this book.

---

[14] This is, on my opinion, the most plausible of all philosophies.

The wisdom gain is a part of post-traumatic growth that arises from the experience of a tragedy (ibid.). Thereby comes also a better understanding of life and also the motive to live life more abundantly (ibid.). So salutogenic components can also arise (ibid.).

2.4.2. PITT - Psychodynamic Imaginative Trauma Therapy

Because of the lack of space, here only the most famous type of trauma therapy here in Germany may be mentioned that involves the researching of positive psychology – PITT – Psychodynamic Imaginative Trauma Therapy.

2.4.2.1 Treatment Steps in Therapy

Main components of the PITT-process are as follows (summarized):

- Building of trust and relationship
- Transference and countertransference
- Identifying and confronting trauma and trauma processes
- Recognizing and preventing a perpetrator-victim-offender development
- Resource orientation
- Building of self-determination, dignity and resilience
- Emotion control – emotional intelligence
- Imagination exercises
- Rehabilitation
- Integration phase (Reddemann, 2011).

In such a therapy process, both approaches are obviously available: psychoanalysis and positive psychology, but also other resource-oriented approaches. This is an integration model example of how one can reconcile multiple approaches.

2.5. Research on the Subject of Positive Psychology in Trauma and War Trauma Therapy

The condition of working successfully with traumatized people is to enhance their intelligence and attention to be able to see the broader and positive picture. Various studies with positive feelings show why it is important to expand the attention.

> "Scientists at Brandeis University in Boston, Massachusetts, succeeded in verify our discovery that positive emotions also increase people's attention, by means of the method of sight movement registration (eye-tracking)" (Fredrickson 2011, p. 82).

The same research shows that negative sentiment, triggered by aversive and repulsive images, nullify even the increased attentiveness (Fredrickson 2011). Therefore, it is important to control the therapy process consciously and to restrict negative images and memories.

For a trauma, it is crucial how someone remembers their past – happy or proud, fiercely or coyly; it depends on memories (Seligman, 2007). Memories are the main source of present feelings and also of mental state (ibid.). Positive memories create life satisfaction, negative memories about it, especially in regard to the injustice of the perpetrators, create negative feelings, even anger and vengeance (Seligman, 2007). To improve satisfaction with life, it is important to emphasize good memories about the past and to emphasize the following: their intensity, their frequency and their labeling (ibid.). The only way to help our brain to get rid of the negative emotions is through forgiveness, forgetfulness, or suppressing negative experiences (Seligman, 2007). There is no well-known direct way in which ideas and memories can be intentionally deleted (Seligman, 2007). For example, an attempt not to think of a white bear for the next 5 minutes doesn't work (ibid.). As well, it is very hard to forget unjust deeds and events. On the other hand, there are several reasons why many victims want to forgive their perpetrators:

> „Forgiving is unjust. It undermines the motivation to catch and punish the perpetrator, and it saps the righteous anger that might be transmuted into helping other victims as well.
>
> Forgiving may be loving toward the perpetrator, but it shows a want of love toward the victim.
>
> Forgiving blocks revenge, and revenge is right and natural" (Seligman, 2007, p. 75).

Forgiveness can transform your own bitterness in neutral or even positive memories, which can lead to the overcoming of a trauma and to life satisfaction (Seligman, 2007). According to the researches, especially in the cardiovascular area, it was shown that a person who forgives survives much better, than a person who can't do that – a contradiction between lack of forgiveness and life satisfaction (ibid.). Other researches, however, show that forgiveness after huge experiences of violence and strong emotional wounds even have a negative impact on health (Lopez & Snyder, 2011, p. 454). In each individual contrition, social support plays a crucial role, whether the victims should forgive the offender, or take revenge on him (ibid.). The extent to which someone is ready to forgive a misdeed is dependent on the personality structure, value system and severity of the deed (ibid.). The whole area is still a new field in psychology (Lopez & Snyder, 2011). Therefore, the question of forgiveness should be treated carefully.

In the chapter on positive psychology the results and important moments of the main research in the field of trauma and especially of the war trauma were so listed:

- Work on a positive adaptation to new circumstances,
- Work on positive feelings,
- Development of character strengths and virtues,
- Work on the resilience- and post traumatic growth building,
- Working on a positive meaning of life,
- Finally, work on a self-renewal in the therapy.

Through various experiences of working with traumatized patients, this methodology of positive psychology in war trauma therapy has achieved considerable success (Joseph & Linley, 2006).

2.5.1. Resilience

A term which inevitably occurs in the context of trauma therapy is »resilience«. It includes mental toughness, originally coming from the Latin term »*resilio*« - "I jump back" - "to discover renew the previous state of well-being." (Reddemann, 2011, p. 28). It is determined "from the relationship between risk and protection factors" (ibid.), or between traumatic stress and the protective reactions. Nevertheless, in every man can a boundary of the trauma burden be higher than the strength of resilience. Therefore, the task of therapy is to create a higher maximum level of resilience, so that the psyche of patients must not suffer unnecessarily (ibid.).

Some pioneers of resilience research are:

• **Aaron Antonowsky** in his research about the »**Salutogenesis**«, the doctrine about the origin of health (Reddemann, 2011).

• **Emmy Werner and Ruth Smith** with their »**Kauhai-research**« (ibid.).

• **Mihaly Csikszentmihalyi** with his ten-year research »**flow**« (Csikszentmihalyi, 1993) – "the form of happiness, over which we have control" (Huhn, 2011), and other (Reddemann, 2011, p. 28).

• In addition also »**traumatic growth**« by **Joseph and Linley** from recent neuropsychological research (Joseph & Linley, 2008).

All of these research areas go into the course of mental health building and not in the direction of any disease. These studies raise questions:

> "How do people achieve, despite costs, to stay healthy or become healthy again? What do mentally healthy individuals do, what could less healthy learn from them?" (Reddemann, 2011, p. 28).

This is the challenge of each trauma therapy and also of this study. Although the goal of trauma therapy is an improvement of the mental health of patients, resilience doesn't mean necessarily "[...] a long-lasting sense of well-being, but **resistance** [highlight - DM]" compared to mental stress (ibid.). The Bielefeld research by Losel and employees shows the decisive resilience factors:

> "[...] active management efforts, cognitive skills, experiences of self-efficacy, positive self-esteem, flexibility and above all, strong emotional relationships" (Reddemann, 2011, p. 29).

To have a resilient attitude means to accept crises because "[...] the energy is thereby released, which is otherwise used for internal strife" (Reddemann, 2011, p. 30). But a person needs time to develop something like this optimistic and predictive attitude without blaming him-/herself constantly (Reddemann, 2011, p. 30).

The modern personality psychology may refer to such people as resilient, who show one of the three most common big-five personality profiles,[15] namely with low neuroticism

---

[15] A model of personality psychology, which analyzed five factors and main dimensions of personality: Neuroticism, extraversion, openness to experience,

value and slightly above average values in other four dimensions: extroversion, openness to experience, agreeableness and rigidity / conscience (Robins et al., 1996; cited in Wikipedia, 2012).

> "In the Longitudinal study of Asendorpf and van Aken (1999) resilient children were described by their teachers as adaptable, resilient, attentive, efficient, clever, curious, and full confidence" (Wikipedia, 2012).

2.5.1.1. Researches on Resilience

Various studies make it clear that resilient people adapt themselves more easily to changes, "in the face of expected threats get less worried and recover faster" (Fredrickson, 2011, p. 138).

> "Such people respond to what is happening now and not on the what if. They are not wasting any effort worrying about the future. Instead, they take a waiting attitude and assume that they will somehow cope with the challenges awaiting them. […] They minimize their fear thus concealing worries and fixed ideas and instead they concentrate on the reality of the present moment" (Fredrickson, 2011, p. 138).

They also try to find something good in the bad (ibid.). The contrast to resilience is called »vulnerability«, with the meaning that somebody is more easily injured by external influences, which increases mental and physical illnesses (Wikipedia, 2012).

Continued from previous page

---

agreeableness and conscientiousness (Wikipedia, 2012).

To measure the personal resilience feature, the American psychologists Jack Block and Adam Kremen from the University of California have developed a resilience scale (ER89) after over five decades of research with 14 points to test, "how normal people cope with the ups and downs of life" (Fredrickson, 2011, p. 128). Herewith was especially the willingness tested to be engaged in something new (Fredrickson, 2011). Among others, the feelings in unpleasant situations of life were examined. With people with resilience there was particularly remarkable positive attitude towards life (Fredrickson, 2011). Thus, they succeed in keeping a higher degree of optimism, calmness and relaxation even after severe life strokes, or even to develop these virtues (ibid.).

Another investigation in the lab, in connection with negative "threats" (simulated by repelling images), has clearly shown through a cardiovascular examination, that such people recover faster (Fredrickson, 2011). The brain activity was scanned before and after the stressful situations and it was found, that resilient people have experienced relaxation faster. It is particularly striking that there were no differences between the two trial groups in their reactions while watching the repulsive images – only during the recovery phase (Fredrickson, 2011). This means that there is no emotional distance in the resilient people. Also resilient people struggle with negative emotions such as fear, anger and grief (ibid.). "But in the midst of their suffering and their worry, they experienced some positive feelings" (Fredrickson, 2011, p. 130). They have experienced "joy, love and gratitude when they were together with other people" (Fredrickson, 2011, p.

130). They have recovered even faster in cardiovascular and brain activities (ibid.). "People with a resilient personality worried less, which in turn meant a faster relief" (Fredrickson, 2011, p. 130). This allows a faster adaptation to changes in such people (ibid.). This is a summary that represents their attitude to life:

- Such people appreciate the now, and are able "to find something good even in the bad" (ibid.).

- They hope for a positive future (ibid.),

- Their positive attitude protects them from the downward spiral of depression and allows them inner growth despite their problems and suffering (ibid.).

The terrorist attack in New York on September 11, 2001 was a fitting occasion for resilience research. Barbara L. Fredrickson, the Professor of psychology at the University of North Carolina at Chapel Hill, United States, has tested a group of about 100 college students on resilience before the terrorist attacks. After the attack she wanted to check the same group now how they have overcome this serious crisis and to examine to what extent the previous resilience values are now effective (Fredrickson, 2011). The test procedure was performed by means of the resilience questionnaire of Block & Kremen, by various surveys about their emotions after the terrorist attack to measure the character traits that are responsible for a person's mental toughness (Fredrickson, 2011). Their psychological strength, including optimism, their serenity and their life satisfaction were also measured (ibid.). Students, who had high values of resilience and thus a resilient personality type, have proved themselves to be resistant even after the terrorist attack (Fredrickson, 2011). They have recovered faster than others with lower resilience (ibid.).

> "In some respects, they developed even greater mental strength after the terrorist attacks. They were more optimistic, calm and felt their life as fulfilled. People with a resilient personality obviously get better more rapidly than the rest" (Fredrickson, 2011, p. 129)

This has confirmed that resistant people recover faster in such difficult situations, because they have greater emotional flexibility and complexity (Fredrickson, 2011). A positive life attitude is obviously accompanied by resilience and helps the troubled individual to recover more quickly from setbacks (Fredrickson, 2011).

This research has clearly shown that resilient people also struggle with the same negative emotions like all others: with anger, fear and sadness (Fredrickson, 2011). In addition to equally negative feelings, they also have concern and sympathy for the relatives of the victims (ibid.). Together with other suffering people, resilient students have experienced joy, love, and gratitude too (ibid.). These moments of positive feelings were responsible for the fact that they have to cope with their negative emotions (Fredrickson, 2011). Thus the already announced theory of Fredrickson was confirmed, that positive emotions and basic attitudes are resilience promoting (ibid.).

In stressful situations, they concentrate not on the negative feelings; they hold on to the positive ones (Fredrickson, 2011). Their emotions are complex, so their positive attitude comes parallel in addition to negative emotions (ibid.). Resilient people use their best resources in difficult situations (Fredrickson, 2011).

What **physical response differences** make such people resilient? – Fredrickson's lab studies show that fear can increase our blood pressure (Fredrickson, 2011). This study has shown, however, that our nerve system has a »reset-button« to delete the negative feelings and to lower high blood pressure: this »button« is our positive feelings (see: Fredrickson 2011, S. 133f). They can lessen negative reactions and slow down their heart rate (Fredrickson, 2011). Also a positive attitude helps to slow down the negative feelings (Fredrickson, 2011). This discovery, if applied, can help many people with heart disease with a psychosomatic basis (ibid.). People without a resilient personality structure have problems with the heart beat frequency (ibid.).

Another study by Dr. Christian Waugh, conducted with the procedure known as magnetic resonance imaging (fMRI), shows how structures of thought and brain activities differ from each other in resilient and non-resilient people (Fredrickson, 2011, p. 136). Heart rate and blood pressure alongside their insular cortex were recovering and normalizing after a negative experience faster in people with a resilient personality structure (Fredrickson, 2011).

A second result has shown that in the resilient experimentees the brain activity in the region of the orbitofrontal cortex (OFC), responsible also for worries, has shown less activities in the unpleasant symbols-phase of the study (Fredrickson, 2011).

A third result of this study showed: the stronger the excitement "about a possible negative experience" was, the slower and longer the recovery (Fredrickson, 2011). Because resilient people have become less worried, they could recover more quickly (ibid.). The difference was not in reactions with unpleasant impulses, but in the emotional dynamics (Fredrickson, 2011) – **resilient people show a greater mental flexibility.**

An interesting model of resilience is developed through empirical research with several children:

Competence or Adaptation Level

	Low		High
Low	highly vulnerab ility		competen t/ unchallen ged
High	maladaptive		resilient

(left axis label: **Risk or adversity Level**)

Figure 6: Resilience model ("Figure 6.3"),
(Lopez & Snyder, 2011, S. 80)

"Full diagnostic models of resilience classify children on the two major aspects of individual lives: good outcomes and adversity/risk. **Figure 6.3** illustrates this model. In the Project Competence study of resilience (Masten et al., 1999), this strategy was used to complement the variable-focused analyses. Figure 6.3 a full diagnostic model of resilience that identifies groups by two sets of criteria for (a) **adversity level** and (b) good outcome or **competence** on one or more criteria. Of greatest interest are comparisons of the "corner" groups: the **resilient**, who are high on both adversity and good outcomes; the **maladaptive**, who are high on adversity but have negative outcomes; the **competent/challenged**, who are low on adversity with good outcomes; and the **vulnerable**, who do not do well even though adversity is low" (Lopez & Snyder, 2011, p. 80).

2.5.1.2 Resilience Improvement

Resilient people distinguish positive from negative thoughts and emotions very well (Fredrickson, 2011). This is no self-evident ability. It can and should be developed and learned by patients.

Due to the studies presented, it follows that to increase resilience, the patient's positive quotient (positive feelings in relation to the negative - 3-1) should be increased (Fredrickson, 2011). This growth possibility is empirically determined by the degree of resilience at the beginning and at the close of the study (Fredrickson, 2011).[16]

Within a month it could be already determined that positive emotions increase the resilience degree (Fredrickson, 2011). Also experimentees with a lower degree of resilience were able to react more openly to emergency situations with the help of accompanying encouragement and have achieved a positive attitude (ibid.). Also people with the most difficult life blows have succeeded in replacing their fears and negative

---

[16] Such a questionnaire is available on the website: www.PositivityRatio.com.

thoughts with positive ones through an active keeping of "[...] joy, joyfulness, inspiration and pride in their everyday life [...]" (Fredrickson, 2011, p. 141). Unfortunately, not all patients were able to develop resilient skills. That is the problem of any therapy, counseling and pastoral care.

For both a faster physical and mental recovery, it is important to maintain contact with everything that is resilience-stimulated:

• with nature,

• with positive oriented people,

• with positive memories (of beloved people, places, activities and events),

• with aesthetics and beauty,

• with pleasant sensory stimulants (taste, smell, music...) and

• with everything that affects the psyche positively (Fredrickson, 2011).

Affected by trauma, people have greater needs, mostly for loving support. As a result, the task of trauma therapy, counseling or pastoral care is to analyze the situation of patients systematically and to find practical solutions to meet their specific needs. Cooperation with family members can be a great support in therapy, to develop the openness of patients to others, which may be very useful for the suppression of the bonding on trauma.

To develop the resilience strength of the individual merely personal inner strength is not sufficient; a supportive social network of the whole social community is necessary (Fredrickson, 2011). Positive feelings are important not only within a person, but also between people. Positive words and actions have a very positive influence on the heart and cause positive feelings for the needy (Fredrickson, 2011). The resulting upward spiral brings people closer to each other (Fredrickson, 2011). Contrastingly, a negative downward spiral carries a sufferer down a dark and lonely road, into deep isolation from the community of helpful people (ibid.).

Another difference between resilient and non-resilient people lies in the basic way of reacting to current problems: in despair or in hope (Fredrickson, 2011). Despair increases negative feelings such as fear, uncertainty, stress, grief and shame (ibid.). This downward spiral can very quickly lead to the absolute abyss of destruction (Fredrickson, 2011). The setting of hope, however, is constructive, solution-oriented and opens new positive perceptions inside (ibid.). It leads to a faster recovery from negative experience events, an increase of resource analysis (ibid.).

It seems that genetic predisposition plays also an important role in resilience (Fredrickson, 2011). Such genetically predetermined resilient people are commonly known as optimists. Even in the most difficult situations, they maintain good feelings (Fredrickson, 2011). Nevertheless, everyone can develop optimism. According to positive psychologists, an optimistic and positive attitude to life is genetically predisposed in all humans (Fredrickson, 2011, p. 146). For that reason, they believe, that everyone already has this ability (ibid.). The »tipping point« between the inner lethargy and flowering mental health, like between the ice and the water (0° C), is the 3-to-1-quotient – "a magic number in human psychology", is actually a natural law of human psychology (Fredrickson, 2011, p. 149). This is an average ratio of three times more positive against the negative feelings, thoughts and experiences. This means that one should deliberately exercise to maintain positive, resilience promoting moments and constructively overcome the negative ones.

When it refers to couples, the tipping point is even higher. John Gottman, a leading marriage expert, came through his empirical research in his "marriage laboratory" to the positive quotient 5:1 (five positive experience related events to one negative in the marriage), as the key to the success of the marriage (Fredrickson, 2011, p. 161).

Also the scientist Robert Schwartz came to similar results. He has measured this quotient in depressive patients every week before and after the treatment period with questionnaires about their feelings, treated either medically or with a cognitive behavioral therapy (Fredrickson, 2011). Every two weeks an independent medical team assessed them (ibid.). The positive ratio of 4.3 to 1 applied to the patients who were completely relieved of depression (Fredrickson, 2011, p. 162). With the patients with an average success the ratio was 2.3 to 1 (Fredrickson, 2011). With the not healed patients their positive ratio after the treating was 1:1 (ibid.).

Thus, various independent studies show that e.g. in work teams, or in a partnership, it is important that positive feelings and experiences may at least three times exceed the negative ones (Fredrickson, 2011). This quotient is also a tipping point under which the value of the positive feelings is not so effective (ibid.). In weaker values positive feelings for such people are "useless and ineffective" (Fredrickson, 2011, p. 164). Positive emotions, however, have enabled openness and growth (Fredrickson, 2011). This is also the ultimate point where the perspective either narrows or extents (ibid.).

Scientific evidence clearly shows that negative feelings and experiences have a damaging effect; consequently, the question arises thereupon: why should such negative elements in life not be avoided completely? If the positive ratio of 3:1, or even 5:1 is healthy, why could not 100:1 be an ideal? (Fredrickson, 2011).

On the other hand it is a fact that this is absolutely impossible on this earth (Fredrickson, 2011). Negative emotions have a legitimate place in each constellation in our lives. After a loss, it is appropriate to mourn, in a danger to feel fear, or in face of injustice to feel anger and resentment (ibid.). Appropriate negative feelings make us honest and real and very often they protect us from dangers. People can hardly understand each other without such experiences. In life, it is often confirmed that an exaggeratedly, positive attitude brings new problems (Fredrickson, 2011). This is obvious if children live only with love and nice experiences, they are often very spoiled and selfish. Both in childhood and adolescence such people have no sympathy and compassion for others. They don't comprehend the suffering and have no sympathy for suffering people. Even in many people who prefer only joy and fun there is very often a lack of responsibility and creativity (so-called "Joker"). Although lasting negative feelings and experiences work negatively, they are a normal part of life. So, the clear distinction between **appropriate** and

inappropriate negative emotions should be made (Fredrickson, 2011). John Gottman has found through his research,

> „[…] that anger and strife can be healthy and productive forms of negativity, while abhorrence and disrespect rather destructive effect" (Fredrickson, 2011, p. 166) .

Negative emotions and attitudes go very deep and dominate the whole emotional structure of life and lead to a downward spiral (Fredrickson, 2011). On the other hand, it is not possible to solve all problems only with kind words. That's why positive and negative feelings must be brought into a balance similar such as weightlessness and gravity (Fredrickson, 2011). This can be so achieved that the corrective and energizing feelings may be separated from destructive ones that can lead to pathological conditions (such as: depression, phobias, obsessive-compulsive disorder, etc.) (ibid.). A useful scientific method to keep negative thoughts and emotions under control is first to analyze them. Helpful questions could be something like following:

- "How did they [these negative thoughts - DM] develop?
- What did this trigger in me?
- How much does this idea represent my reality?
- How does the situation actually look like?
- How do I feel when I look only at facts?" (Fredrickson, 2011, p. 194).

It is very important "to question the distortions of negative thinking" (ibid.). A healthy logic with the right priorities and common values helps in this matter. For example, the family is more important than any success; life and health are more important than work, or possessions, etc. If one fights against negative thoughts with healthy arguments, they will be removed in the blossom (Fredrickson, 2011).

By the asking of questions, it is important to avoid endless ruminations and unnecessary worry, because they multiply negative feelings and finally result in panic attacks (Fredrickson, 2011). To achieve that, it is important to recognize the unnecessary negativity immediately as it appears and to do something that improves the mood (ibid.). Every human being has their favorite activities that generate joy, fascination and satisfaction (ibid.). This helps to get a clear view, because only then will it be possible to solve real problems constructively (ibid.).

To consider negative feelings methodically from an emotional distance can be done through mindfulness. In this way, you can teach depressed and traumatized people about a new self-validating and way of thinking visually. From the standpoint of Bible-oriented pastoral care it is »sinful human nature«. Sin (evil), according to the Bible, came into our world through one man, Adam, and so into all people who have genetically inherited it through him.[17] This is exposed through genetic errors or mutations. Many inherited diseases (including mental illnesses) and deformations bear witness to this fact,

---

[17] Rom. 5:12 "Therefore, just as sin came into the world through one man, and death through sin, and so death spread to all men because all sinned" (English Standard Version Bible, cited from http://biblia.com/books/esv/Ro5.12 on April 27, 2014).

that every human being has errors (mutations and degenerations). Since the genes determine not only our body, but also our psyche (through the nerve system) any man, according to the Bible, is far from being in original healthy state (all are "corrupted")[18] and therefore their own thoughts and feelings must be repeatedly questioned and checked as to whether they are positive or negative. To be honest, despite everyone's efforts to behave consistently either to their own or to society's principles any human justice is far from the righteousness of God according to the Bible.[19] No one is without sin and therefore nobody has the absolute right to judge or to condemn others.[20] Therefore, a complete change – spiritual rebirth is necessary to belong to the Kingdom of God already here now and in the future.[21] This spiritual, inner change is similar to the mental transformation as for example, in cognitive therapy in psychotherapy. A new mindset,

---

[18] Apostle Paul summarizes the biblical doctrine of the sinful human nature in the Roman 3:10: "as it is written: "None is righteous, no, not one; 11. no one understands; no one seeks for God. 12. All have turned aside; together they have become worthless; no one does good, not even one" (English Standard Version Bible, cited from http://biblia.com/books/esv/Ro3.9 on April 27, 2014).

[19] Romans 10:3 "For, being ignorant of the righteousness of God, and seeking to establish their own, they did not submit to God's righteousness" (English Standard Version Bible, cited from http://biblia.com/books/esv/Ro10 on April 27, 2014).

[20] Luke 10,37 "Judge not, and you will not be judged; condemn not, and you will not be condemned; forgive, and you will be forgiven;" (English Standard Version Bible, cited from http://biblia.com/books/esv/Lk6.37 on April 27, 2014).

[21] John 3:3 "Jesus answered him, "Truly, truly, I say to you, unless one is born again he cannot see the kingdom of God" (English Standard Version Bible, cited from http://biblia.com/books/esv/Jn3.3 on April 27, 2014).

perspective and the attitude towards other people and the whole reality is necessary in every psychotherapy / counseling. That's why parallels between biblical pastoral ministry and psychotherapy are apparent.

Only the path to the solution is different. Almost in all psychotherapy schools (about a hundred), patients do everything alone in their mental strength with the help of therapists. In pastoral care, however, the only way to get back to the original healthy nature – the original image of God in human[22] – is through the gradual transformation of the character. This moment is very similar to positive psychology, which emphasizes the character very strongly. The characteristics are very identical in both approaches. Only the way to do this is slightly different. The ideal in positive psychology is a virtuous character, which has nothing to do with a personal God. The man can reach that through psychological training and psychotherapy. Pastoral care, however, has as a goal the perfect example of Jesus Christ that is to be achieved through the spiritual consideration of his wonderful character and life. The perfect ideal is supernatural and outside of man. Therefore, the example of Jesus Christ in addition to all psychological approaches is very important in the Christian ministry. How Christ perceived people, how he dealt with them, how he endured the suffering and how he understood the whole reality, etc. If his model is used in pastoral care in a reasonable and balanced way, then many

---

[22] Gen. 1:27 "So God created man in his own image, in the image of God he created him; male and female he created them." (English Standard Version Bible, cited from http://biblia.com/books/esv/Ge1.27 on April 27, 2014).

difficult questions and moments can be treated more easily and finally the emotional healing can be achieved more easily. Of course, the clear differentiation between his divine nature / abilities and our human ones should be clearly defined, not to fall into the "messianic syndrome".

A very important moment in Christian pastoral care is the influence of the Holy Spirit, who is actually the secret of the inner, spiritual strength of the people (resilience). He gives all necessary inner character traits and skills necessary for a positive life.[23] On the one hand, it is not possible for humans alone to achieve this superior goal.[24] On the other hand, the Spirit of God causes gradually through the spiritual change that which is not possible for us humans.[25] This positive change, resilience, is a result of the cooperation of the pastoral minister and client with God.

The end result of such therapy/counseling/pastoral care and especially in the case of an integration of pastoral ministry with psychotherapy, i.e. an integrative concept, would be much more than just a healing of mental disorders and

---

[23] Gal. 5:22 "But the fruit of the Spirit is love, joy, peace, patience, kindness, goodness, faithfulness, 23 gentleness, self-control; against such things there is no law" (English Standard Version Bible, cited from http://biblia.com/books/esv/Ga5.22 on April 27, 2014).

[24] Romans 7:18 "For I know that nothing good dwells in me, that is, in my flesh. For I have the desire to do what is right, but not the ability to carry it out" (English Standard Version Bible, cited from http://biblia.com/books/esv/Ro7.18 on April 27, 2014).

[25] Matthew 19:26 "But Jesus looked at them and said, "With man this is impossible, but with God all things are possible" (English Standard Version Bible, cited from http://biblia.com/books/esv/Mt19.27 on April 27, 2014).

illnesses. With such a complete approach patients can share a higher **spiritual** nature – the divine one.[26] They get to know the logic and the mind of God.[27] The complete transformation of the whole person, including **physical** transformation, will happen according to the Bible one day at the Second coming of Christ – so-called "glorification".[28] This is actually the biblical / Christian higher sense of life – to be ethically now and in the future also physically similar to God. At the moment, there is compatibility between pastoral care and positive psychology:

> "A life that does this is pregnant with meaning, and if God comes at the end, such a life is sacred" (Seligman, 2007, p. 258).

It is clear that such a psychic/spiritual concept in full scope would be possible only to spiritually open patients. Anyway, even with people who are not spiritually oriented you can have this orientation in the mind to make greater contribution to them than only treating problems.

---

[26] 2 Peter 1:4 "by which he has granted to us his precious and very great promises, so that through them you may become partakers of the divine nature, having escaped from the corruption that is in the world because of sinful desire" (English Standard Version Bible, cited from http://biblia.com/books/esv/2Pe1.4 on April 27, 2014).

[27] 1 Cor. 2:16 "For who has understood the mind of the Lord so as to instruct him?" But we have the mind of Christ." (English Standard Version Bible, cited from http://biblia.com/books/esv/1Co2.16 on April 27, 2014).

[28] Phil. 3:21 "Who will transform our lowly body to be like his glorious body, by the power that enables him even to subject all things to himself" (English Standard Version Bible, cited from http://biblia.com/books/esv/Php3.21 on April 27, 2014).

2.5.2. Mindfulness

The trauma condition analysis (see the chapter "Trauma") has shown that negative feelings and memories greatly limit the positive insights and findings of positive life moments (Fredrickson, 2011). Traumatized people are often so fixated on their suffering and grief that they can neither see nor learn the positive matter. Concentration training should help this. The required method for this is **mindfulness training**.[29] Though thousands of years old and mostly practiced by different Far-Eastern meditation practices, scientific researches of the 20th century have detected that it is not only a pure spiritual practice from Asian culture, but is an effective capability of our mind (Fredrickson, 2011). There are various mindfulness exercises also in therapy. In positive psychology and pastoral care you can practice positive experiences that develop positive feelings and thoughts in clients:

- o through the exchange of positive experiences with beloved people,
- o through the exchange of physical or mental photos
- o through the narration about the positive experiences
- o or through the expression of gratitude for the

---

[29] "[...] Form of open-minded attention that focused on the present moment and meet it without prejudice" (Fredrickson, 2011, p. 139). That means "[...] to give to inner experiences full attention, without judging them" (ibid., p. 200). "The power of mindfulness is able to literally tear the band between negative thoughts and negative feelings" (ibid., p. 201).

positive gifts in life (Seligman, 2007).

Fredrickson recommends the "metta-meditation"[30] by which you "try to wake positive feelings in the context of our relations [...and] can increase the feeling of love and care for yourself and for your fellows" (Fredrickson, 2011, p. 235).

In pastoral care, gratitude to God can be expressed for everything that is good and positive in life.[31] Positive exchange is also possible by different faith themes, discussions, dealing with case-related Scriptures, also by learning of such encouraging texts and above all through prayer (in a group or alone). Research on the practical consequences of such spiritual practices is recommended in psychotherapy / counseling as well as in the field of pastoral care.

2.5.3. Post Traumatic Growth (PTG)

Although the trauma general and especially the war trauma can leave severe and long-lasting post-traumatic stress disorder (PTSD), it is noted in practice, as well as in empirical research, that some people can grow psychologically from traumatic experiences. Tedeschi and Calhoun have developed the first theoretical scientific definition (Tedeschi & Calhoun, 1995, 1996, 1998, 2004, cited in Zöllner, Calhoun & Tedeschi, 2006, p. 37).

---

[30] Developed by Sharon Salzberg (Fredrickson, 2011, p. 293).

[31] Colossians 3:15 "And let the peace of Christ rule in your hearts, to which indeed you were called in one body. And be thankful" (English Standard Version Bible, cited from http://biblia.com/books/esv/Col3.15 on April 27, 2014).

"Post-traumatic growth means positive psychological changes in those affected as a result or consequence of the management process with extremely stressful life events. The term posttraumatic growth emphases that sufferers not only recover from the trauma, but they use it as an opportunity for continued personal development. They report about an increase in inner maturity, newly defined sense of life and positive changes in their own person" (Zöllner, Calhoun & Tedeschi, 2006, p. 37).

Numerous studies have founded the undisputed growth following traumatic event types:

"These include sadness and loss experiences after the death of family members and partners (Calhoun & Tedeschi 1989-1990, Davis et al., 1998, Edmonds & Hooker 1992, Hogan et al. 1996, Lehman et al. 1993, Miles & Crandall 1983, Nerken 1993, Schwab 1990), rheumatoid arthritis (Tennen et al. 1992), HIV infection (such as Bower et al. 1998, Schwartzberg 1993), cancers (such as Collins et al. 1990, Cordova et al. 2001), bone marrow transplantation (Curbow et al. 1993), heart attacks (Affleck et al. 1987), accidents (Joseph et al. 1993), house fires (Thompson 1985), sexual assaults (Burt & Katz 1987, Frazier et al. 2001) and sexual abuse (McMillen et al. 1995), war experiences (Elder & Clipp 1989) and held hostage by (Cole 1992) " (Zöllner, Calhoun & Tedeschi, 2006, p. 38)".

Post-traumatic growth has different levels that can manifest themselves differently in different areas of life (ibid.). Until now, five areas of personal growth have been discovered that can help also in the therapy:

1) **Intensified appreciation of life** – a person learns to appreciate the essentials in life, but also to enjoy the small things in life (Zöllner, Calhoun & Tedeschi, 2006);

2) **Intensified relationships** – through the support after a trauma, sufferers come closer to other people, so that relations are gaining in importance. Very often a growth of compassion for other people develops, especially for those in need (Zöllner, Calhoun & Tedeschi, 2006). On the other hand a distancing and avoidance of them that give no support can begin (ibid.);

3) **Awareness of own strength** – in difficult situations people learns to know their own strengths and weaknesses (vulnerability). Both dimensions grow out of disaster: both the realization that unpleasant events can come at any time, as well the certainty how to cope with them due to positive experiences (Zöllner, Calhoun & Tedeschi, 2006);

4) **Discovering of new opportunities** – due to unpleasant changes positive opportunities also emerge – growth in social engagement, learning a new profession, new experiences, new friendships, etc. (ibid.);

5) **Intensified spiritual awareness** - through personal maturity is also a new spiritual awareness of the higher and broader context of life (Zöllner, Calhoun & Tedeschi, 2006, p. 38).

For the practical work with these five areas Maercker & Langner (2001), designed an interview guide for the German version of the self-assessment questionnaire "Post traumatic personal maturation" (German: "Posttraumatische

Persönliche Reifung" – PPR). It was made based on the five subscales. The interview looks like this:

"Introductory questions:

Could you describe the event to us? When did it take place? How did you live in the days after that, how were the first months afterwards?

Let me go with you in the course of the interview to some areas, in which something may has changed for you.

Discovery of new opportunities:

Do you live your life differently... have you developed new interests? How would you describe your way of life, do you believe to live another life… [Do you have] since then new ways that were previously not possible to be realized? Are you now more willing to change things that need to be changed?

Awareness of own strength:

Was self-confidence developed more as a result (and how you have become stronger as a result), do you now handle difficulties or changes differently?

Intensified relationships:

How have the relationships with others changed? Did relations become more important? How does the relationship with your family look like when compared to previously? (Connectedness – to do so others can be included).

Can you put yourself in the position of others? Can you express now more feelings towards others, which you kept before the accident to you?

Intensified appreciation of life:

Do you have new ideas in regard to what is important and what are priorities in life? What is important to you now compared to before in your life? Would you say that you live the days now more consciously?

Intensified spiritual awareness:

What is faith for you?
Did the faith or philosophy of your life change? Has it now a different significance in your life?

Final questions:

What has changed most for you?
What did good to you?" (Scherer, Stocker, Rottensteiner & Beck, 2011, p. 14-17).

A paradox arises from the whole traumatic experience – "A gain arises from a loss" (Zöllner, Calhoun & Tedeschi, 2006). Herewith grow the life wisdom and experience (ibid.). What can be also very helpful is development of gratitude. It is quite difficult to develop gratitude after traumatic events; nevertheless, it might be a great help, to see new possibilities and alternatives:

> "An attitude of gratitude may be one means by which tragedies are transformed into opportunities for growth, being thankful, not so much for the circumstance but rather for the skills that will come from dealing with it. The ability to discern blessings in the face of tragedy is a magnificent human strength" (Lopez & Snyder, 2011, p. 467).

Research by Coffman (1996) with 13 parents residing in South Florida after the disaster of Hurricane Andrew in 1992 discovered, that also, during the period of the greatest losses, people could be grateful for what they have not lost (Lopez & Snyder, 2011).

This concept differs from other positive concepts, such as resilience and optimism in the fact that no existing positive personality traits are needed for post-traumatic growth (Zöllner, Calhoun & Tedeschi, 2006).

> "In contrast to that, post-traumatic growth refers to transformative or qualitative changes that exceed the pre-traumatic development level of mental functioning and the consciousness of a person. These are significant positive changes in cognitive and emotional abilities and experience, that can be linked to behavior implications" (Zöllner, Calhoun & Tedeschi, 2006, p. 39).

Post-traumatic growth (PTG) is a theoretically different concept. Some theorists regard it as result of the **trauma management process** (Schaefer & Moss, 1992, 1998; Tedeschi & Calhoun, 1998, 2004; cited in Zöllner, Calhoun & Tedeschi, 2006, p. 39). Others, however, see it as a **coping**, or coping model, as an adaptive strategy of finding the meaning (Davis et al., 1998, Park & Folkman, 1997, cited in ibid.) or as an **explanation model,** why the trauma has happened (Filipp, 1999, cited in ibid.).

The prerequisite for the development of the individual growth process is experiencing an event so distressing that previous assumptions no longer match with reality and that existing management skills can no longer be sufficient (Zöllner, Calhoun & Tedeschi, 2006). This causes a machine-like process, which is firstly characterized by an automatic rumination ("chewing") of the negative experiences, which gradually merges into a conscious reflection about the trauma and its significance (ibid.).

Although rumination in clinical psychology means more thinking, Tedeschi and Calhoun (2004) recently prefer the term »cognitive processing« (Zöllner, Calhoun & Tedeschi, 2006). The main element of personal growth is the "[...] Degree of conscious reflection about the trauma and the perception of personal income (benefits)" (Zöllner, Calhoun & Tedeschi, 2006, p. 40). From personal characteristics openness and extraversion seems [32] necessary to be a support force for new experiences and the PTG (Tedeschi & Calhoun, 1996, cited in publication, Calhoun & Tedeschi, 2006, 40). This also includes the individual social system that can promote and develop new patterns and approaches (ibid.).

It is useful to ask in the section for medical history for specific changes that go in the direction of mental maturity and post-traumatic growth (Reddemann, 2011). This can help to lead patients in a positive direction at the beginning of the therapy/counseling – to draw their attention to the positive moments in their experience and to encourage them to look for the positive moments in their lives.

All these results are a scientific confirmation of the phenomenon of spiritual growth through suffering in Christian pastoral care and spiritual life. There are several examples in the Bible where people have grown through enormous suffering and afflictions:

---

[32] "Extraversion is "the act, state, or habit of being predominantly concerned with obtaining gratification from what is outside the self" (Merriam Webster Dictionary)" (Wikipedia, 2014).

- A particularly striking example is Joseph, one of the twelve sons of Jacob, father of the nation of Israel. Out of strong jealousy of Joseph's special status and preference of the father, his brothers sold him to Ishmaelites as a slave.[33] Joseph loses not only his high status as future heir, but also his whole family, his home and everything he had. So he remained as a slave in Egypt. However, the Lord is with him and blesses everything he does and gives him prosperity.[34] After a period as a slave to the army general Potiphar, Potiphar's wife tries to seduce him.[35] Unfortunately, on one occasion she succeeds in accusing him of the "attack"[36] because of his loyalty to God

---

[33] Genesis 37,27."Come, let us sell him to the Ishmaelites, and let not our hand be upon him, for he is our brother, our own flesh." And his brothers listened to him. 28. Then Midianite traders passed by. And they drew Joseph up and lifted him out of the pit, and sold him to the Ishmaelites for twenty shekels of silver. They took Joseph to Egypt" (English Standard Version Bible, cited from http://biblia.com/books/esv/Ge37.27 on May 01, 2014).

[34] Genesis 39,2 „The Lord was with Joseph, and he became a successful man, and he was in the house of his Egyptian master. 3 His master saw that the Lord was with him and that the Lord caused all that he did to succeed in his hands. 4 So Joseph found favor in his sight and attended him, and he made him overseer of his house and put him in charge of all that he had. 5 From the time that he made him overseer in his house and over all that he had, the Lord blessed the Egyptian's house for Joseph's sake; the blessing of the Lord was on all that he had, in house and field. 6 So he left all that he had in Joseph's charge, and because of him he had no concern about anything but the food he ate." (English Standard Version Bible, cited from http://biblia.com/books/esv/Ge39.2 on May 01, 2014)

[35] Genesis 39:6 "…Now Joseph was handsome in form and appearance. And after a time his master's wife cast her eyes on Joseph and said, "Lie with me" (English Standard Version Bible, cited from http://biblia.com/books/esv/Ge39.4 on May 01, 2014).

[36] Genesis 39:11 "But one day, when he went into the house to do his work and none of the men of the house was there in the house, 12 she caught him

and to his master and so he goes to jail and remains there several years, seemingly as a hopeless case.[37] However, because God blesses him, he is prosperous also in this situation and has success.[38] After some time it happens, that he should interpret two very impressive dreams before the Pharaoh and also to recommend how to react to them. Impressed by the wisdom and understanding of this young man, the Pharaoh chooses Joseph as his co-regent over the whole land of Egypt.[39] So, despite all traumatic experiences he

Continued from previous page

---

by his garment, saying, "Lie with me." But he left his garment in her hand and fled and got out of the house. 13 And as soon as she saw that he had left his garment in her hand and had fled out of the house, 14 she called to the men of her household and said to them, "See, he has brought among us a Hebrew to laugh at us. He came in to me to lie with me, and I cried out with a loud voice. 15 And as soon as he heard that I lifted up my voice and cried out, he left his garment beside me and fled and got out of the house." 16 Then she laid up his garment by her until his master came home, 17 and she told him the same story, saying, "The Hebrew servant, whom you have brought among us, came in to me to laugh at me. 18 But as soon as I lifted up my voice and cried, he left his garment beside me and fled out of the house." (English Standard Version Bible, cited from http://biblia.com/books/esv/Ge39.11 on May 01, 2014).

[37] Genesis 39:19 "As soon as his master heard the words that his wife spoke to him, "This is the way your servant treated me," his anger was kindled. 20 And Joseph's master took him and put him into the prison, the place where the king's prisoners were confined, and he was there in prison" (English Standard Version Bible, cited from http://biblia.com/books/esv/Ge39.13 on May 01, 2014).

[38] Genesis 39:21 "But the Lord was with Joseph and showed him steadfast love and gave him favor in the sight of the keeper of the prison. 22 And the keeper of the prison put Joseph in charge of all the prisoners who were in the prison. Whatever was done there, he was the one who did it. 23 The keeper of the prison paid no attention to anything that was in Joseph's charge, because the Lord was with him. And whatever he did, the Lord made it succeed" (English Standard Version Bible, cited from: http://biblia.com/books/esv/Ge39.21 on May 01, 2014).

has grown, to the highest position in the whole Kingdom rather than falling into a deep depression. This is a very clear biblical example of traumatic growth.

-You can see similar cases involving many other persons in the Bible: Moses, the Prophet Elijah, King David, the Prophet Daniel, Jesus Christ, the Apostle Paul, and many others. These people in Bible history have sometimes unendurable difficulties, but they have grown from them and have become stronger. Apostle Paul brought it together:

> 2 Corinthians [**12.10**] "For the sake of Christ, then, I am content with weaknesses, insults, hardships, persecutions, and calamities. For when I am weak, then I am strong" (English Standard Version Bible, cited from: http://biblia.com/books/esv/2Co12.10 cited on May 01 2014).

As a young man I personally could not understand these words previously. Later, through many life difficulties that I have experienced, I could become stronger and more

Continued from previous page

---

[39] Genesis 41:37 "This proposal pleased Pharaoh and all his servants. 38 And Pharaoh said to his servants, "Can we find a man like this, in whom is the Spirit of God?" 39 Then Pharaoh said to Joseph, "Since God has shown you all this, there is none so discerning and wise as you are. 40 You shall be over my house, and all my people shall order themselves as you command. Only as regards the throne will I be greater than you." 41 And Pharaoh said to Joseph, "See, I have set you over all the land of Egypt." 42 Then Pharaoh took his signet ring from his hand and put it on Joseph's hand, and clothed him in garments of fine linen and put a gold chain about his neck. 43 And he made him ride in his second chariot. And they called out before him, "Bow the knee!" Thus he set him over all the land of Egypt. 44 Moreover, Pharaoh said to Joseph, "I am Pharaoh, and without your consent no one shall lift up hand or foot in all the land of Egypt" (English Standard Version Bible, cited from: http://biblia.com/books/esv/Ge41.37 on May 01, 2014).

determined. Maturity, experience and security are the after-effects of such life challenges. Although, these are not always beneficial, yet everyone can grow and mature through difficulties.

Finally, this applies to the whole of humanity. We all (with few exceptions) have to fight with many problems in this life, including diseases, injustice and negative experiences with other people – what is everyday life for many people. However, as a result we learn to deal with these problems successfully and grow from them. For the apostle Paul it is an inner growth.[40] Finally, one day all winners in this battle of life will get a very high position from the ruler of the universe – to rule with him over the entire universe.[41] People who have experienced the worst (persecution, violent death, etc.) get the judicial positions in the Kingdom of God.[42] The roles are here

---

[40] 2 Corinthians 4:16 "So we do not lose heart. Though our outer self is wasting away, our inner self is being renewed day by day. 17 For this light momentary affliction is preparing for us an eternal weight of glory beyond all comparison," (English Standard Version Bible, cited from: http://biblia.com/books/esv/2Co4.16 cited on May 01 2014).

[41] The glorified Jesus promises to his church in Laodicea and to all winners:

Revelation 3:21 "The one who conquers, I will grant him to sit with me on my throne, as I also conquered and sat down with my Father on his throne" (English Standard Version Bible, cited from: http://biblia.com/books/esv/Re3.21 cited on May 01 2014).

[42] Revelation 20:4 „Then I saw thrones, and seated on them were those to whom the authority to judge was committed. Also I saw the souls of those who had been beheaded for the testimony of Jesus and for the word of God, and those who had not worshiped the beast or its image and had not received its mark on their foreheads or their hands. They came to life and reigned with Christ for a thousand years" (English Standard Version Bible, cited from:

changed and finally perfect justice will win. The guarantee for that is the resurrection of Jesus Christ to heaven[43] as the representatives of the righteous in the Heavenly Court.[44] It seems in the Bible as if the negative experiences in this life function as training, or preparation for the ruling position in eternity. Although this may be in the long-term future, a suffering person can be empowered, still in this life, to help others in similar situations.

2.5.4. Real Positive Effects of Trauma

No one can deny the negative consequences and losses caused by trauma-, especially war trauma experiences, which good therapists, counselors, or ministers should never overlook. Nobody can ever replace lost family members, friends, children, or eventually lost parts of the body. This should be recognized in therapy. You cannot undo what has happened. In pastoral care, especially with unprofessional comfort, there is a danger in trying to find an explanation for suffering and for what has happened and to represent all that as the will of God. This would be counterproductive. The other

Continued from previous page

---

http://biblia.com/books/esv/Re20.4 cited on May 01 2014).

[43] Acts 17:31 "Because he has fixed a day on which he will judge the world in righteousness by a man whom he has appointed; and of this he has given assurance to all by raising him from the dead" (English Standard Version Bible, cited from: http://biblia.com/books/esv/Ac17.31 cited on May 01 2014).

[44] Hebrew 8:1 "Now the point in what we are saying is this: we have such a high priest, one who is seated at the right hand of the throne of the Majesty in heaven," (English Standard Version Bible, cited from: http://biblia.com/books/esv/Heb8.1 cited on May 01 2014).

extreme is "[...] that traumatic experiences are always growth-stimulated. They are not,..." (Reddemann, 2011, p. 48).

In the trauma processing also develop which positive effects, according to various experiences and scientific research, are real (Zöllner, Calhoun & Tedeschi, 2006). They should be distinguished from self-deception methods of pseudo-maturation (such as: "If it had already to happen, then it must be good at least for something", ibid.). There are scientific critics who represent post-traumatic growth as a form of defensive illusion (Wortman, 2004, Lechner & Antoni, 2004; Maercker & Zöllner, 2004; cited in Zöllner, Calhoun & Tedeschi, 2006, p. 40);

> „[…] but there are people who succeed in achieving profit from an extreme affliction for themselves and their maturation. And to be interested in, and not, to exclude, these experiences, is in the interest of those patients who have such opportunities" (Reddemann, 2011, p. 48).

Also pastoral care has to achieve similar goals. To sum up, positive psychology deals with a real positive development of posttraumatic treatment to see how persons with a trauma can be even more resilient, wiser, more mature and positive.

2.6. Christian Counseling/Pastoral Care

The term »counseling« was already long established regardless of the Christian values. Nevertheless, Christian counseling and pastoral care are the oldest type and their origin. Counseling is "the oldest component of pastoral cares and has a proven tradition, as well as a central priority in the churches" (Nestmann, 2007, p. 155). Pastoral care is actually the oldest type of counseling. The term itself comes not from the Bible, yet in practice it is biblical (Klessmann, 2008). It is also known as "life counseling", which actually belongs to the pastoral care (Nestmann, 2007a, p. 155). Psychology, psychotherapy and counseling have actually evolved out of the Christian counseling and pastoral care and have taken over their sole claim of jurisdiction a long time ago (ibid.). While there may be sometimes tension and rivalry with pastoral care,

> "Each has a range of its own competence, in that the other does not intervene: i.e. the psychotherapist recognizes the competence of the pastoral care when it comes to the question of relationship with God. The pastor acknowledges the competence of psychotherapy when it comes to dealing, for example, with 'claustrophobia'" (Herbst, 1999, p. 6).

Cooperation and mutual support is recommended. Some pastors are trained as psychotherapists and counselors, or alternatively – psychologists, psychotherapists and counselors can complete a pastoral training. Such phenomena are still a rarity on European soil. It is good to understand that the soul (psyche) is important, but the perhaps even superior spiritual area as well. For many people, their faith is the basis of their attitude to life and of their worldview.

Translated into computer language, the faith would be comparable to a main operating system, by which all other installed programs are connected to each other. However, without an operating system, all programs would be useless. On the other hand, good programs, e.g. these for Windows, are not compatible with all operating systems, e.g. with Macintosh and vice versa. Therefore, it is important to adapt good applications/programs to the main operating system.

Similarly to that, psychology, psychotherapy and common non-Christian counseling are mostly ineffective in terms of faith without theology- and faith understanding. For this reason, Christian pastoral care has a unique role in the spiritual field, which no other discipline can replace. It is an operating system, where not all psychological and therapeutic approaches are compatible and can be installed. In **cases of spiritual issues and needs** of the patients, it is recommended to recognize one's own limits as a therapist or a counselor and to transfer the client to an appropriate pastor. The optimal combination would be to have actually training in both skills.

Although Christian pastoral care is very comprehensive, it touches general human experiences as: family, "parenting, partnership, employment, ageing, disease and health" (Klessmann, 2008), spiritual and ethical issues (ibid.), encouragement, active listening to the suffering ones; briefly summarized – the sympathy to fellows and solidarity (Klessmann, 2008). It has as a goal "to strengthen the life and the certainty of faith of people" (ibid.).

The unique element in Christian counseling is the relationship between the pastor and the clients based on the "authenticity, condition-free value estimate (which Rogers identified as "love" in the sense of biblical Agape) and empathy (see John 8:32; Roman 15:7; Heb. 5:2.)" (Nestmann, 2007a, p. 159).

2.6.1. Relationship Between Christian Pastoral Care and Positive Psychology

In the European zone there is hardly any researching comparing Christian pastoral care with positive psychology. One reason may be historical. On the one hand, in Europe psychology in general, as well as psychotherapy, is atheistic-materialistic and therefore secular-oriented. The foundation of today's modern psychology is set in late 19th century together with the natural sciences (physics and chemistry) (Clinton & Hawkins, 2011). All scientific knowledge was enriched solely on the basis of empirical research. All religious values and contents about human nature and people's psyche are thus excluded (Clinton & Hawkins, 2011). All ideas about God, righteousness, sin, and the fall were therefore excluded (Clinton & Hawkins, 2011). In this way social science disciplines have been apart and detached from theology and pastoral care. Since Freud's time, the psychology generally has a very skeptical attitude towards religion:

> "For a half century after Freud's disparagements, social science remained dubious about religion. Academic discussions of faith indicted it as producing guilt, repressed sexuality, intolerance, anti-intellectualism, and authoritarianism" (Seligman, 2007, p. 57).

On the other hand, this has caused a distance by Christian pastors and theologians. General psychology and pastoral care a good relationship did not have for a long period of time. In the United States, on the contrary, the Christian psychology emerged gradually, which is based on the foundation of Christian belief (Clinton & Hawkins, 2011). Their interest is also in empirical research and theoretical definition, which has to do with the Christian understanding of biblical theological teachings and ideas of Christian philosophy about human nature. Accordingly, Christian psychology also uses terms such as God, sin and salvation (see Charry, 2010; Evans, 1990; Johnson, 2007; Roberts & Talbot, 1997, cited in Clinton & Hawkins, 2011, p. 25).

Over the last 20 years the non-Christian scientists have performed empirical research on the influence of faith on health, which has shown positive results in psychological fields:

> "Religious Americans are clearly less likely to abuse drugs, commit crimes, divorce, and kill themselves. They are so physically healthier and they live longer. Religious mothers of children with disabilities fight depression better and religious people are less thrown by divorce, unemployment, illness, and death. Most directly relevant is the fact that the survey data consistently show religious people as being somewhat happier and more satisfied with life than nonreligious people" (Seligman, 2007, p. 57).

2.6.1.1. Positive Psychology on Spirituality

In the United States positive psychology has a good relationship with spirituality and pastoral care, particularly in the context of trauma. The following text explains the thinking of positive psychologists towards spirituality:

> "[...] we think, what is especially worth drawing attention to is that of religious change and the question of the relationship of spirituality to growth (see Shaw, Joseph,

& Linley, 2005, for a review). As Lyons notes, spiritual issues are hard to avoid in trauma therapy, and yet we know very little about the role of religion and spirituality in growth. As Mahoney, Krumrei, and Pargament (Chapter 6, this volume) explore, the relation between spirituality, stress, and growth is not a simple one, with the potential for spiritual beliefs to be either strengthened or shattered following trauma" (Joseph & Linley, 2008, p. 348, 349).

Faith is an important force for trauma relief; however, its influence on the recovery from the trauma in psychology is until now not yet explored empirically enough:

"Thus, further qualitative research in this area that seeks to understand the different factors that drive the strengthening or shattering of spiritual beliefs following trauma would be fruitful" (Joseph & Linley, 2008, p. 349)

An open mind attitude towards positive psychology, especially in the United States, is growing in Christian circles. A Conference of the »Christian Association for psychological of studies (CAPS)« in Kansas City, 15-17 April 2010 entitled »Abundant Life« made a contribution to the connection between the positive psychology and Christian pastoral care. For example, Rod Hetzel, Ph.D., "the chair of the positive psychology section of APA division 17" (Christian Association for Psychological Studies, 2010) has launched a workshop titled »Positive Psychology and Clinical Practice«, with the following objectives:

"Learning objective 1: participants will be able to articulate a framework for integrating positive psychology within a broader Christian worldview,

"Learning objective 2: discuss areas of convergence and divergence between positive psychology and Christian spirituality" (Christian Association for psychological of studies, 2010, p. 2)

Positive psychology has an important place in the framework of studies in many universities (about thirty in the United States) and includes its own compartments on positive psychology (altogether 45) (positive psychology Center, 2007) in recent times to be taught also in Christian universities, for example in the American Graduate University, Washington, United States (Regency University, 2010). It also occurs gradually in the footsteps of Christian counseling (Collins, 2012). It is an important topic at Conferences of the Society for Christian Psychology, such as the biannual Conference of the Society for Christian Psychology at Regent University, Virginia Beach, VA (in October 18-20, 2012) (Koinonia, 2011). Recent development of an integrative concept have been conceived with the name »**Christian Positive Psychology**« (by Nancey Murphy in "Why Psychology Needs Theology: A radical reformation perspective")[45] (Dueck & Lee, 2005, cited in Hakney, 2007, p. 211). Obviously the integration of positive psychology with Christian thought is developing. For this area more research and development are needed, because positive psychology itself is a psychological discipline in further development. Therefore the combination

---

[45] Murphy tries to put the neo Aristotelian ethical philosophy of MacInture as a metatheoretic basis for a structure of a mainly Christian program of psychological research and practice (Hakney, 2007). His wish was also to develop a new integrative perspective – to connect the positive psychology with the pathology and mental disorders (Hakney, 2007).

of these two approaches is not to be overlooked for theologians, ministers and counselors. Because the required space for a detailed and long investigation is not sufficient here in this book, I want to examine only in brief sketches a comparison between the basic elements of the positive psychology and the principles of the Christian theory, which can be used as a good complement and deepening of the Christian pastoral care or counseling:

2.6.1.2. Similarities Between Positive psychology and Christian Pastoral Care

• **Positive emotions** are strongly emphasized in positive psychology (Fredrickson, 2011) and are in accordance with all noble emotions of Christian character (Phil. 1:11; 4:8). Also positive social emotions and bindings are in accordance with Christian charity (Mt. 19:19; 22:39) and the positive life- or basic attitude (Ecclesiastes 9:7);

• **Positive character traits** – virtues and strengths in positive psychology (Seligman, 2007), (see the figure 4: "Classification of the 6 virtues and 24 strengths" on the page 48), are a confirmation of the Christian emphasis on the positive character. This is much exalted in the Bible – "a virtue" (Philippians 4:8), or the "fruit of the spirit" (Galatians 2:22,23) that make us "partakers... of the divine nature" (2 Peter 1:4). All six virtues[46] of positive psychology are actually parts of the biblical concept. A very similar list is also available in 1 Peter 1:5:

---

[46] Wisdom, courage, love for humanity, justice, moderation, and spirituality/transcendence (Seligman, 2007).

"5 For this very reason, make every effort to supplement your faith with **virtue**, and virtue with **knowledge** *[wisdom *in the pos. psychology* - DM]*, 6 and knowledge with **self-control** *[moderation* - DM]*, and self-control with **steadfastness** *[higher level of moderation* - DM]*, and steadfastness with **godliness** *[spirituality / transcendence* - DM]*, 7 and godliness with **brotherly affection**, and brotherly affection with **love** *[philanthropy* - DM]*" (English Standard Version, cited from: http://biblia.com/books/esv/2Pe1.4 on May 7, 2014, bold - DM).

This list is missing only righteousness, which according to the Bible is included in philanthropy (Romans 13:9.10). The similarity and compatibility of these two approaches is obvious.

• The Bible has an even broader list of noble character traits (Galatians 5:22.23). All associated 24 character strengths are fully in line with the Christian image. To analyze this a complete study is required;

• To **engage positively** and **constructively** for the benefit of one's own and the wider human family (Seligman, 2007) is also in accordance with the Christian idea of service to fellow men, which is emphasized even more in Christianity – as an expression of the love of Christ (Matthew 25:31-40; John 13:34) and with the biblical principle of efficient work (Ecclesiastes 6:6-11), to which belongs the merit of prosperity in Germany and Europe;

• The emphasis on the **life-meaning** (Seligman, 2007; Joseph & Linley 2008) as the basis of a positive life is also in accordance with Christian thought. The difference is that positive psychology sees humans only as beings developed in the chain of evolution who should only complete their development. The Bible, however, sees humans as God's children, godlike beings, with the **higher meaning of life** as rulers over the Earth (Genesis 1:26-28) clearly defined by the creator of the universe from the beginning of the world (Genesis 1:26). The Bible teaches that this original life meaning was corrupted by sin and should be restored through redemption – in this life through the transformation of the character and life (John 3:3; 1 John 5:4) and then completely one day in the future – by the glorification of humans (1 Cor. 15,51-53) and through the obtaining of the supremacy as co-heirs and co-regents of Christ (Romans 8:17; Revelation 3:21; 22:5). The idea of the Bible for today's life is to live according to this higher life meaning as children of God showing love to each other:

> Eph. [**4.1**] "I therefore, a prisoner for the Lord, urge you to walk in a manner worthy of the calling to which you have been called, 2 with all humility and gentleness, with patience, bearing with one another in love," (English Standard Version, cited from: http://biblia.com/books/esv/Eph4.1 on May 7, 2014).

• The emphasis on **positive interpersonal relationships** (Philanthropy by Seligman, 2007) is a scientific confirmation of the meaning and function of Christian philanthropy and its consequences (Luke 6:34-38). Seligman referred to philanthropy as altruistic (Seligman, 2007), which is actually the condition of following Jesus (Luke 9:23);

• The emphasis on **performance** (»flow«) and on high projects in positive psychology, as an important source of happiness (Csíkszentmihályi, 1993), is in accordance with the all-embracing biblical idea of positive activity in life (Proverbs 14:11; Ecclesiastes 9:9; 1. Thessalonians 4:11.12) and of life perfection (maturity, or enriching of the goal): "You therefore must be perfect, as your heavenly Father is perfect" (Matthew 5:48);

• Understanding of positive psychology, that well-being (happiness) comes not from outside, but depends on **internal conditions** (Fredrickson, 2011; Seligman, 2007), is compatible with the Bible (Philippians 4:12.13), where the idea is very clear, that everything in life is based on spiritual and ethical – internal values (= law of God; Ecclesiastes 12:13.14) applicable for all eternity and significant before God (Romans 2:14-16);

• The emphasis on well-being linked to the **satisfaction** and **gratitude** (Seligman, 2007; Fredrickson, 2011) matches with the biblical idea of satisfaction and gratitude in life (Philippians 4:6);

• Empirical studies in positive psychology that **forgiveness** is very important (Seligman, 2007), is the scientific confirmation of the biblical concept of forgiveness (Luke 23:34; 11:4; 17:3.4) James 3:13);

• The concept of **hope** (Seligman, 2007) is a very strong scientific verification of the meaning and effect of Christian hope that goes even beyond death (John 14:27.28; Acts 24:15);

• The concepts of **resilience** and **personal growth** in suffering and grief (Joseph & Linley, 2008) are the scientific confirmation of the Christian concept of growth through suffering (Romans 5:3-5; James 1:3.4; Galatians 5:22;. 2 Thessalonians 3:5; James 5:11; Revelation 14:12) whereas also grow consolation and encouragement (2 Corinthians 1,3-5; 1 Thessalonians 2:3.4);

• The **critical moment** is **understanding of human nature**. Seligman condemns the doctrine of sinful human nature, which actually includes the basic Bible idea:

> "I call this pervasive view about human nature, which recurs across many cultures, the rotten-to-the-core dogma. If there is any doctrine this book seeks to overthrow, it is this one. "The doctrine of original sin is the oldest manifestation of the rotten-to-the-core dogma..." (Seligman, 2007, p. xii).

This is his negative reaction on the pathology school in the psychology, which actually Freud has established (Seligman, 2007, p. xii). Seligman explains this as follows:

> "I cannot say this too strongly: in spite of the widespread acceptance of the rotten-to-the-core dogma in the religious and secular world, there is not a shred of evidence that strength and virtue are derived from negative motivation" (Seligman, 2007, xiii).

• The focus of positive psychology on the **positive qualities of the human character** is in line with the humanist world view (the same as by Carl Rogers), which itself is positive for the efforts of patients in achieving their own success and can be a good reason to reconsider or supplement trauma therapy, counseling and pastoral care. However, this idea by no means corresponds to the reality in which we live.

2.6.1.3. Differences Between Positive Psychology and Christian Pastoral Care

Despite the obvious similarities and parallels in positive emotions and attitudes, there are also significant differences in relation to human nature between positive psychology and Christian pastoral care.

- For positive psychology, humans are basically good (Seligman, 2007). According to that theory, they lack only the social and psychological competencies that they can develop through the work of personal positive qualities and strengths. That itself is right and necessary in a therapy, counseling and pastoral care. However, according to this idea, humans do not need God to be better. They can redeem or improve themselves. They must only learn how to develop positive emotions, attitudes and character traits. Seen from a Christian perspective, this represents a kind of self-redemption, which the Bible definitely rejects as absurd (see the citation of Seligman on the previous page).

- According to the Bible, however humans are infected by sin not only from the outside, but primarily from within (Matthew 15:18.19) and cannot free themselves with

---

[47] John 15:5 "I am the vine; you are the branches. Whoever abides in me and I in him, he it is that bears much fruit, **for apart from me you can do nothing**.

their own efforts. Seligman, together with the humanistic psychology, categorically rejects this biblical assertion.

- According to the Bible, a deep inner change of the character can be performed thoroughly and permanently only through a higher divine power – by Jesus Christ[47] and by his Holy Spirit who causes all positive changes (John 3:3-8) and not only by psychotherapy / counseling. It's about a »reprogramming« of the human mind, which a person cannot do on his/her own, as well as a computer cannot reprogram itself alone. A programmer must do it – in our case it is the Designer of humans – God the creator. Because this process of a reprogramming includes both – the nerve system (identical to the »hardware«) and our inner world (»software«), that is not possible only through therapy. Therefore cooperation between a therapist / counselor, patient and God is very important.

- This point in relation to human nature should be carefully treated and corrected both within psychotherapy, as well as in pastoral care, not to create any illusion that psychology / therapy was a magic wand with which to help all people. The same also applies to pastoral care – in some cases the clients need in addition to the spiritual care, professional help to recognize and resolve deeply-rooted problems. Therefore, the combined use of both approaches is recommended.

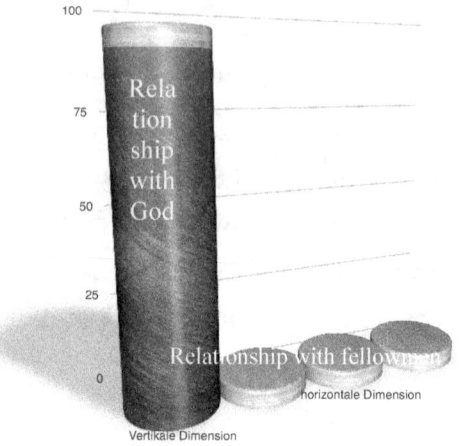

Figure 7: Two dimensions of the pastoral care,
Source: Own source (Author)

- Although positive psychology has recognized the spiritual dimension as one of the most important factors of happiness (one of six character virtues is »spirituality«, or »transcendence«), it does not include this point in therapy. This is not strange, because the founders of positive psychology are all atheists and cannot do this. In the pastoral ministry, however, the ultimate goal is to instill and develop confidence in God and to implement his principles practically in the client's own life, to carry out the necessary changes / healing. **The relationship with God and with other people** is at the heart of pastoral care and at the same time of positive psychology, which has determined that positive relationships are a very strong factor in mental health and well-being (Seligman, 2007). Therefore, working on the relationship between these two dimensions is very important, not only in pastoral care, but also in therapy, where it could be possible, because both dimensions (horizontal and vertical), especially in religious people, exercise their influence on all areas of life.

Although an atheist, Seligman asks questions about God. From them we can learn to understand better the area »Transcendence« in positive psychology. His statements help us in the next chapter.

The claims of Seligman that guilt and shame bring no healing power or correction, but a narrowing of a view and deep vulnerability (Fredrickson, 2011), are partially correct. Accusations, unkindness and unnecessary negativity destroy not only positive emotions but also interpersonal relationships. Nevertheless, there are two types of negativity: "appropriate negativity is specific and correctable. Inappropriate negativity is often just as superfluous as global" (Fredrickson, 2011, p. 166). That's why both in therapy/counseling and in real life, only positive talking and acting cannot be enough, but sometimes limits on the wrong attitude or the wrong action must be clearly defined. Not with each person can you have success only with positive information. Sometimes it is helpful for some people, if you categorically or even critically act against their negative behavior, to represent their actual reality to them (»constructive criticism«, or »appropriate negativity«, Fredrickson, 2011). Only concentrating on the positive does not bring a constructive change in each case. Especially it applies to people with antisocial personality disorder (in DSM entitled as ASPD – people who think they are in the right, while others were all stupid). Friendly speech brings just the opposite in such people. For many offenders, the consequences of their actions were eye opening and useful enough to change their negative attitude to life (prison, failure on its way of crime, etc.).

In this area of the constructive critical analysis of positive psychology, further research is appropriate.

2.6.1.4. Positive Psychology and Belief in God

In relation to faith, positive psychology has a divided setting. On the one hand it originated from the humanist - atheist philosophy – a philosophical empirical attitude towards God, freedom and evil. Their general representation of God is not Christian. This is evident from the following statement:

> "Positive Psychology points the way toward a secular approach to noble purpose and transcendent meaning and, even more astonishingly, toward God who is not supernatural" (Seligman, 2007, p. 12).

Seligman was a prominent psychologist but always an atheist. Most psychologists think that faith means a mental weakness. Nevertheless, it is noteworthy that Seligman thinks on God seriously. He responds to his friend's remark: "I thought you were a nonbeliever" (Seligman, 2007, p. 255) in the following way:

> "I am. At least I was. I've never been able to choke down the idea of a supernatural God who stands outside of time, a God who designs and creates the universe. As much as I wanted to, I have never been able to believe there was any meaning in life beyond the meaning we choose to adopt for ourselves. But now I'm beginning to think I was wrong, or partly wrong" (Seligman, 2007, p. 255).

As an atheist he thinks still about a God who is acceptable for rationalists:

„I have intimations of a God that those of us who are long on evidence and short on revelation (and long on hope, but short on faith) can believe in" (Seligman, 2007, p. 256).

For Seligman, a meaningful life is finally abundance of that which has to do with God:

"A meaningful life adds one more component: using these same strengths to forward knowledge, power, or goodness. A life that does this is power, or goodness. A life that does this is pregnant with meaning, and if God comes at the end, such a life is sacred" (Seligman, 2007, p. 258).

The main problem for trained people like Seligman and his colleagues is the problem of evil. They cannot relate the problem of free will, the omniscience and omnipotence of God with the reality of evil, which is generally difficult for all people. That's why they have immense problems believing in an almighty and merciful God who allows so much evil and suffering. Many deep thinking people have the same problem.

This brief analysis shows that there are many good ideas in positive psychology that are very applicable also in Christian pastoral care. Ethical and social values are almost identical. Other equivalents with positive psychology are visible in valuable spiritual values such as character, hope, love, etc., as a scientific confirmation and practical deepening of the Christian teaching about character. So their ethical values are to be recommended as a method of amplification of the psychological immune system, which can serve not only against all negative experiences and problems, but also to an expansion of a happy life and personality within pastoral care and therapy.

2.6.2. Pastoral Care and Resilience

Although resilience can be a personal (inherited) quality, it is possible to learn it – everyone can learn and grow in behavior, thoughts and activities (Higgins 1994, cited in Lopez & Snyder, 2011, p. 166). Research by Higgins (1994) shows that some people who have experienced severe suffering, have become much stronger then they could have imagined (Lopez & Snyder, 2011). To build resilience in pastoral care means instead of discussing fully about the trauma and weakness, one should rather consider the development of mental resistance, which effectively promotes personal capabilities (ibid.). There is always a danger to focus ourselves on problems and healing of psychological damage ("the damage model", Wolin & Wolin, 1993, quoted in ibid.), rather than on the personal and ultimately family strengths.

In the process of resilience development in traumatized people it is important to recognize both – protective and risk factors. Risk factors such as low self-esteem, addiction dependence, sexual abuse, etc., have a very negative effect on problem-solving strategies and consideration of alternative situations (Lopez & Snyder, 2011). The protective factors in pastoral care enhance self-esteem and develop self-protection measures:

> „Protective factors include faith, morality, a sense of
> humor, insight, independence, the ability to connect/attach
> to others appropriately to form relationships, initiative, and
> creativity (Ungar & Liebenberg 2008; Peters, Leadbeater &
> McMahon, 2010). These resiliencies form a framework that

gives individuals and families an edge in combating adversity" (Lopez & Snyder, 2011, p. 167).

It is very important to ensure support for the people seeking advice – as in the therapy/counseling process, as well as in the social environment (ibid.), especially by involving members of the family. However, the most important contribution of the pastoral care is building confidence in God and strengthening both hope and faith in the divine guidance in all situations (Proverbs 3:5.6; 1. Peter 5:7). This includes the exploration of personal strengths and experiences, where God has given the necessary power and blessing to the person. This leads to the realization of the strength, resilience and responsibility to solve problems and trust in God and to modify their own behavior (Lopez & Snyder, 2011).

> „As clients begin to recognize that amid their problems they also have God-given strengths, they are able to harness hope and confidence that healing and restoration can happen for them. The result is a demonstration of competence and an escape from lifelong mental distress.

> Frequently, individuals are unaware of their resiliencies and either ignore or downplay them. But as counselors listen to clients' narratives, they can identify resiliencies and, through open-ended questioning, help clients discover the manifestations of these qualities. Helping clients reframe their stories to include application of their faith and belief in their identity in Christ catapults the ability to identify strengths, resiliencies, and responsibilities, and it ultimately leads to improved problem solving and a change in their behavior. Resilience is the picture of one's faith lived out in the midst of difficult circumstances, supported by moral and

conscientious decision making" (Clinton & Hawkins, 2011, p. 167).

For this purpose, the questions concerning suffering in the context of the grace and power of God are very important:

- What does God think about human suffering?
- Where is he in such moments?

It is important to emphasize that God does not cause suffering, but he allows it, because he has given to humans free will to decide either for or against him. According to the Bible, the Designer of the Universe has created the first man as the ruler of the Earth to have a chance either to acknowledge his Supreme rule, or not – including the consequences that follow afterwards. Freedom is sanctity for God and that's why he consistently keeps the law of free will. And here is a very difficult problem also for Almighty God. How can he protect humans, prevent suffering and still allow the freedom of all those involved in our sinful world? How may he merge himself in the life of those who are not on his side? These conditions are very often unclear and difficult to understand for us humans. Therefore, we cannot understand his apparent absence in many difficult situations.

Yet, although he does not prevent sufferings in most cases (because he keeps the law of free will), he uses them to lead people to a higher level of spiritual maturity to defeat evil. To do this he uses life crises, helping us to experience his love and help even deeper then in normal situations (Lopez & Snyder, 2011). Often spiritual crises help to correct the incorrect understanding of God, negative life attitudes, or to restore the abandoned faith (Lopez & Snyder, 2011). The best example of spiritual resilience was the patriarch Job, who trusted God despite the worst losses and blows of fate (Job 19:25-27). He has not understood his situation and why he had to endure all sufferings. Yet he has seen finally, that he cannot understand it, because it exceeds his understanding:

> Job 42:3 "'Who is this that hides counsel without knowledge?' Therefore I have uttered what I did not understand, things too wonderful for me, which I did not know."

Finally, he has expressed his confidence in God and expressed his willingness, to be instructed and led by him (Job 42:2-6).

The Apostle Paul reveals the secret of the inner resilience and strength with the following statement:

> Ephesians 3:14 "For this reason I bow my knees before the Father, 15 from whom every family in heaven and on earth is named, 16 that according to the riches of his glory he may grant you to be strengthened with power through his Spirit **in your inner being**, 17 so that Christ may dwell in your hearts through faith — that you, being rooted and grounded in love," (English Standard Version, cited from http://biblia.com/books/esv/Eph3.14 on Mai 8, 2014, [bold – DM]).

The resilience that the Apostles of Jesus have shown came not from their own strength, but from the Holy Spirit, which has given them superhuman vigor. Therefore, cooperation with the Spirit of God is very important in the pastoral care / counseling process. This maturation process cannot be only emphasized by the pastoral care, but also practically encouraged – in the midst of difficulties to help the clients to recognize the love of God for the suffering ones. To do this, it is good to strengthen the loving support of family and of the friendship circle, to be able to identify and to experience positive elements in the midst of difficulties.

It is good also to show the dealings of God with the suffering of the patients – this is reflected particularly by the example of Jesus Christ. He entered in our world, became a human and suffered voluntarily in our human nature because of our mistakes, to grant us the freedom from evil and eternal life. As well as all resilient people, he was not happy to suffer – his three prayers in Gethsemane show that clearly too.[48] However, he adopted and deliberately allowed sufferings, to gain a higher goal – the salvation of mankind. Despite the inhumane suffering, he has endured the unbearable because he has done everything with a higher sense of life. His example has given to many Christians a superhuman strength to endure terrible suffering and injustice without losing their mind (especially in persecutions and war times) or to be offenders (»introjection«). Therefore, the original Christianity has an inspirational force for successful pastoral care and counseling.

2.6.3. Research on the Impact of Faith on Health

When traumatized people are open to faith, various biblical life stories can be interesting to them, how trust in God, even in trouble, can boost happiness. The "secular"

---

[48] Mathew 22:42 "saying, "Father, if you are willing, remove this cup from me. Nevertheless, not my will, but yours, be done" (English Standard Version, cited from http://biblia.com/books/esv/Lk22.42 on Mai 8, 2014).

history hardly mentioned the word "happy" in the context of the traumatic experience. However, you can find such reports in the sacred history of the Bible, as in the following examples:

- Report on Josef, the son of Jacob, of Israel's Patriarchs, in captivity, after a serious traumatic experience of betrayal by his brothers and capture to Egypt, "The Lord was with Joseph, and he became a successful man, and he was in the house of his Egyptian master (Genesis 39:1, English Standard Version – cited from: http://biblia.com/books/esv/Ge39.1 on Mai 8, 2014);

- It was reported about the future King David that in the midst of the traumatic experiences of the murder trials of the king Saul against him: "And David had success in all his undertakings, for the Lord was with him." (1 Samuel 18:14; English Standard Version – cited from: http://biblia.com/books/esv/1Sa18.14 on Mai 8, 2014).

- About the Prophet Daniel is also recorded in a similar way– despite the earlier traumatic experience of spending a whole night in the lion pit, it is documented: "So this Daniel prospered during the reign of Darius and the reign of Cyrus the Persian" (Daniel 6.29, English Standard Version – cited from: http://biblia.com/books/esv/Da6.27 on Mai 8, 2014). Despite all the difficulties Daniel, instead of post-traumatic disorder, developed the "flow" and growth in his life.

Many people have had such experiences, among them also myself, that the positive belief in God even in the midst of highly traumatic experiences, can give a release and "experience of happiness" with the confidence that God can help and accomplish everything positive. In a possible further study, such surveys can make an important contribution to this research.

Nevertheless, each pastor and Christian counselor may become aware of today's reality. In the 21st century new challenges come for pastoral care, requiring a new emphasis and approaches. A huge challenge for the Christian Counseling and pastoral care is present and constantly changing...

> "Life and work in the post-modern society, the associated need for flexibility and the need for lifelong learning in the midst of an ideological pluralism of previously unknown proportions" (Nestmann, Das Handbuch der Beratung 1, 2007, p. 156 [translated by DM]).

An increasing secularization of society in Europe also causes the loss of interest in church life and at the same time increases a critical attitude toward churches generally (Nestmann, Das Handbuch der Beratung 1, 2007, p. 156). On the one hand, the loss of confidence in Christian counselors and pastors increases. On the other hand, the religious or spiritual needs for security, for a sense of life, for hope and for a secure future grow. That's why, despite all negative developments in society in relation to the general atmosphere towards churches, it is very important to create an integration of the various sectors of social care as for example between psychology, psychotherapy, counseling and Christian pastoral care. Also medicine can be helpful in this integration, which is also appropriate for the diagnosis of some problems, as well as for solutions in the treatment process. Although psychologists and counselors do not necessarily need to study medicine, a general medical knowledge is recommended to regard and handle people as a union or wholeness of the soul, spirit and body. The same applies to a general knowledge of theology/pastoral care, to be able to understand and guide people with various religious backgrounds and styles better. As the basis of pastoral care I recommend primarily **good knowledge of the Bible**, together with **a personal relationship with God**.[49] It requires a life challenge to gain new experiences, but the results are tremendous blessings.

2.6.3.1. Clinical Reviews of Spirituality

New scientific research has shown that there are more and more clinical evaluations on faith and spirituality. Numerous studies are pursued in the United States concerning of the question as to how much faith and spirituality have a positive influence on health. Many of them point out that an active spiritual life can reduce not only mental stress and depression, but can prolong life up to 6.6 years (Utsch, 2011). This is true only for a positive relationship with God. Believers who are burdened with fear and guilt are equally as sick as average people or even more so (Utsch, 2011).

One of the greatest psychology researchers who have combined faith with psychology, as a harbinger of the positive psychology, was a believer – Viktor Frankl (born on March 26, 1905 in Vienna; died on September 2, 1997) (Wikipedia,

---

[49] In the case of interest and questions about that, you can write me on the e-mail on the end of this book.

2012). In his best selling book (9 million copies) under the title »...And still say yes to life« he demonstrates his experience in four Nazi concentration camps with a summary, "that the spirit determines the body, that the spirit uses the body as a tool" (video interview with Viktor Frankl: Frankl, 2010). His positive belief has given him power to endure the sufferings and torture in the concentration camp (along with the loss of his entire family) and to develop a positive perspective in worst situations:

> "There is actually no single life situation or suffering situation which would not have any opportunity to convert them into a meaningful performance" (Video interview with Viktor Frankl: Frankl, 2010).

In the recent times there has been more and more research into the influence of faith on health. The following is a brief summary published in 1998 in the newspaper "Focus":

> "More than 1200 independent investigations have confirmed the observation in the past few years that religiosity may be an effective treatment. People who believe in a higher power are less often in hospital, recovered faster from illnesses, have lower blood pressure and seem better protected against cardiovascular diseases. They are also faster again on their legs after surgery and need less analgesics" (dpa/Demography, 2005).

How does faith specifically affect human well-being? How does a positive belief specifically influence health according to the results of scientific research?

2.6.3.2. Faith and Health – Specific Effects and Results

Research on the influence of faith on health in 1968 at Harvard University (United States) under the direction of Herbert Benson has shown that meditation, or prayer reduces the stress hormones[50] and their consequences, reduces a too strong secretion or even completely prevents it (Benson, 1998). Other research has shown that meditation and prayer can be effectively used in treating anxiety disorder (Lee, Zaharlick & Akers, 2011; quoted in Clinton & Hawkins, 2011, p. 203). The latest research in natural science confirmed the biblical wisdom (1 John 4:17.18) that love casts out fear (Clinton & Hawkins 2011, p. 203). The following research is also very interesting about prayer and positive emotions in Christian life:

> „The part of the brain in which fear is generated is called the amygdala, whereas the part of the brain in which we experience altruistic love, compassion, empathy, and sympathy is called the anterior cingulate cortex (ACC). Dr. Newberg at the University of Pennsylvania has shown that when individuals aged 60 to 65 meditated 12 minutes a day for 30 days on a God of love, they experience growth in the ACC as measured by MRI brain scans, reductions in heart rate and blood pressure, and improvement in memory testing. Meditating on any other God concept, such as an angry, wrathful, distant, or punitive God did not result in

---

[50] Adrenaline, nor adrenaline, epinephrine and nor-epinephrine (Benson, 1998). These include also corticotropin-releasing hormone (CRH) and adrenocorticotropin (ACTH), cortisol, arginine vasopressins (AVP) (Wikipedia, 2012).

these positive outcomes (Newberg & Waldman, 2009). This means that growth in the ACC from meditating on a God of love calms and reduces the firing of the brains' fear center (the amygdala)" (Clinton & Hawkins, 2011, p. 203).

Such studies in the last two decades show a clear connection between faith and health. One of the founders of positive psychology, Martin Seligman, formulated this as follows:

> „The causal relation between religion and healthier, more prosocial living is no mystery. Many religions proscribe drugs, crime, and infidelity while endorsing charity, moderation, and hard work. The causal relation of religion to greater happiness, lack of depression, and greater resilience from tragedy is not as straightforward. In the heyday of behaviorism, the emotional benefits of religion were explained (away?) as resulting from more social support. Religious people congregate with others who form a sympathetic community of friends, the argument went, and this makes them all feel better. But there is, I believe, a more basic link: religions instill hope for the future and create meaning in life" (Seligman, 2007, p. 57).

The most important and strongest gift, which the Christian faith offers to the community, is hope:

> "The relation of hope for the future and religious faith is probably the cornerstone of why faith so effectively fights despair and increases happiness" (Seligman, 2007, p. 58).

Each support and strengthening of faith through pastoral care, especially in war-traumatized people, is desirable and useful. Therefore, it is of enormous importance for ministers, as well as for counselors and therapists, to deal also with the meaning of faith in the life of the patients. Therefore, I recommend a comprehensive approach in therapy/counseling, greater than ever before – including pastoral care.

2.6.3.3. The Influence of Beliefs on Health

The aforementioned scientist Benson has found in his research on the influence of spirituality on health that our thoughts have a moving power (Benson, 1998). He explains why faith and relationship with God are strong stress-reduction means:

> „Believe in what you know to be important to you, and that belief can definitely counteract the harmful effects of stress. Believe in what you're doing to counteract the stress. Believe in relationships, and if you're of a religious nature, believe in the protective aspects of God. That's good for us because it gives us hope, and that hope is a very wonderful way to cope with many of the stresses of everyday life. Now I'm not saying that we should all believe in God. I'm saying if your belief system is to incorporate God, and that kind of spirituality, that's wonderful. If you're not religious, then use another belief in which you have faith, and that belief can also help you counteract the harmful effects of stress" (Benson, 1998).[51]

Thoughts and beliefs have a powerful force not only in the area of emotions, but also in communicating with our fellow men; they affect our will and finally the whole body (Fredrickson, 2011). Bitterness causes stomach pain, shoulder

---

[51] Website: „Staying Healthy in a Stressful World", 1998, http://www.pbs.org/bodyandsoul/218/benson.htm, seen on April 16, 2012.

and neck muscle tension, even tension in the face muscles (Fredrickson, 2011). This physical tension and pain put the soul into deep exhaustion in the form of negative adjustment – error and guilt are seen everywhere, but no solution (Fredrickson, 2011). It is not surprising that normally a positive mood...

> „[...] is accompanied by lower blood pressure, less pain, less cold illnesses and better sleep. People with a positive attitude are overall less frequently ill. The risks for high blood pressure, diabetes or stroke are much lower. Scientists have already confirmed that a positive mood does extend life" (Fredrickson, 2011, p. 120).

The belief in a loving God who accompanies us in our life despite all terrible experiences and protects us from the inner evil, gives us confidence to proceed on the safe way. The consciousness of sin and Satan causing evil in many people on this earth is a clear understanding of our own suffering and also of the offender's behavior. The only person, who has fully understood this, even in the most difficult moment of his suffering on the cross, was Jesus:

> Lukas 23:33 „And when they came to the place that is called The Skull, there they crucified him, and the criminals, one on his right and one on his left. 34 And Jesus said, "Father, forgive them, for they know not what they do." And they cast lots to divide his garments." (English Standard Version – cited from: http://biblia.com/books/esv/Ge39.1 on Mai 8, 2014)

According to the Bible, blinded by the hypnotic influence of sin and the seduction of Satan, many people often allow themselves to do evil, not conscious of what they actually add to others and also to themselves. Also in the difficult moments of life, which are sometimes absolutely inexplicable, faith produces more patience and confidence in, that perfect justice will finally be restored by the Judgment of God at the very least, at the second coming of Christ. On the matter the meaning of life in difficult moments biblical faith offers the possibility of someday understanding all the reasons why God has allowed something bad. Only through faith can we accept a higher sense of what is not yet fully revealed (included under the title in this book: "IDEAS ABOUT THE HIGHEST MEANING OF LIFE AND SUFFERING").

2.6.4. Christian Counseling and Migration

In Germany, beside private and government organizations, there are also many Christian counseling centers for immigrants, especially in larger cities, mostly in Protestant and Catholic churches and parishes. In Frankfurt am Main the best known counseling center is the »Evangelical Center for counseling and therapy« ("Am Weißen Stein" – translated: "On the White Stone"), with a department "[...] for migrants, as well as counseling and therapy for refugees" (Evangelischer Regionalverband Frankfurt am Main, 2012). Other counseling centers for immigrants and are run by Caritas, Germany. They provide various services according to the needs of the clients. However, the use of positive psychology still hardly exist in them. This is understandable, because it is still new in psychology, psychotherapy and counseling here in Europe. This is a sign of the need for further research and work on integrated positive Christian counseling.

2.6.5. Christian Counseling in War Trauma Therapy

Pastoral care is not a substitute for trauma-, or war trauma therapy, but [...] the first psychological aid in acute emergency situations [...]" (Klessmann, 2008). Klessmann represents pastoral care in four simplified steps:

1. "Identifying symptoms of a traumatic crisis" (Klessmann, 2008, p. 296).
2. "Stabilizing" (ibid.),
3. "Orientation" (ibid.), and
4. "Activate resources" (ibid.).

In the same time it is essential for Christian counselors to develop a trusting relationship with clients.

2.6.5.1. A Relationship of Trust

How to help the traumatized people in the pastoral care? –Confidence in such a context of trauma and war trauma is more important than the methodical approach – even crucial (Reddemann, 2011).

1. Firstly, to create **understanding of the suffering** of the clients. Appropriately, listening understandingly is the golden rule here, as well as in psychotherapy. Listening builds trust with sensible and informative (sometimes "diagnostic") questions (see the "Questions about the biography") and gives a better overview of the whole situation of both parties (Clinton & Hawkins, 2011). The questions should necessarily involve the personal emotional and ethical experience of

clients. Sometimes it is better to conduct an open, unstructured interview, sometimes a less structured one.

2. With a greater confidence it is then important to **convey a positive understanding of life** to clients – a positive sense of life. A big help can be the Bible-oriented sense of life – to develop love of God and of neighbors and to do good. The higher life meaning (the similarly titled chapter in this book) can be a great help to understand the life purpose of us humans.

3. The shared and solitary prayer of clients is a third way of **consolation- and hope earnings**. Therefore, it is important to educate people how to talk with God with confidence and how to gain the certainty, that God hears our prayers regardless of our emotions. This includes also the skill to listen to the voice of God:

- through the Bible,
- through the beauty of nature,
- through positive life events,
- through good people,
- through our conscience
- very often through quiet positive thoughts in everyday life that remind us of the important things.

If open to the voice of God, everyone can learn and experience this skill. I personally use it every day.

Many people, particularly the young and emotional, have problems with faith, while they think: God would not listen to them. According to the Bible, God hears and sees all the thoughts and processes in the whole of nature, as well as in humans. Therefore, there is absolutely nothing that he doesn't hear listen or see. No less important for a trustful relationship with clients is the pledge of secrecy, which is, although not legitimately, but still ethically binding for all ministers. This includes also keeping to the exact time appointments. Proper notice of cancellation in cases of hindrance is also very important. The same rule applies also to clients.

2.6.5.2. Christian Grief Counseling

In each war trauma there comes into being a loss – of security, dignity, property and often of family members. The natural response is sorrow (Shear et al., 2011; Humphrey, 2009, quoted in Lopez & Snyder, 2011, p. 393). It changes the whole life and very often, if too deep and of a longer duration, also the whole personality, which is different in each person (Lopez & Snyder, 2011). Grief comes not only as a response to death or dying, but also from a divorce, loss of employment, by unfulfilled expectations and dreams (ibid.). In the case of war trauma there is very often an accompanying experience of a processing of trauma – as a normal part of life (Klessmann, 2008; Clinnton & Hawkins, 2011). It is a serious phase of life for sufferers, because their main concern is a violent and unjust death of their loved ones. Grief over lost family members, or end-of-life care, is often a challenge for psychotherapists and Christian counselors. It is very important to be open to hear the need of patients and to lead them, if possible, from their trauma to hope in a better future with God now and in the future and to new start in their life in connection with people ready to help them (eventually in a local church or some self-support-teams of war traumatized people).

Acute grief reactions should not be diagnosed and seen pathologically. Grief can be divided into different facets on the grounds of intensity and duration (Lopez & Snyder, 2011); complicated grief can be pathologized, but not acute grief (Shear et al., 2011, quoted in Lopez & Snyder, 2011, p. 393). Although grief is still not listed in DSM-VI-TR, Shear and his colleagues (2011) recommend inserting the complicated grief in DSM-V (Lopez & Snyder, 2011). It is dependent on the different duration and intensity of the loss and of a person, and occurs in 10% of the bereaved (shear et al., 2011; quoted in Lopez & 2011 Snyder, S. 393) predominantly in women (Lopez & Snyder, 2011). The cases of complicated grief are e.g. child loss, suffering from natural or war disasters, or due to violence (Lopez & Snyder, 2011). It is remarkable that children experience grief in a different way to adults (ibid.). In the therapy/counseling of children opportunity should be given to them to express their grief and their loss through pictures or games (ibid.).

In instances of war trauma, it is even more complicated, because brutal events happened in the broader framework of the collective consciousness, causing violence on fundamental values and a loss of physical, mental and spiritual identity (Lopez & Snyder, 2011). The consequences are often in the form of post-traumatic stress disorders but also of all other serious disorders (PTSD), cataloged in ICD-10 and DSM-IV (Lopez & Snyder, 2011). The relatives of traumatized people very often have a secondary traumatization that should be also addressed in counseling and pastoral care (Lopez & Snyder, 2011).

Traumatized soldiers need special treatment, because military life and military culture stigmatize weakness very severely (ibid.). As a result, soldiers experience an additional pressure and a double emotional distress. The proper classification between normalization process of reactions to the stress of military life and to war trauma is a first step towards the solution of the problem using the relevant institutions (ibid.). Nevertheless, war trauma therapy of Bundeswehr soldiers requires special training that mostly only federal military therapists have in the relevant trauma centers have. The therapists / counselors / ministers should be aware of this fact.

2.6.5.3. History of Grief Counseling

The first work appeared in 1972 in the book -"The Process of Grief" (by theologian Yorick Spiegel). Some later, in the 1980s, appeared a book "Grief. Phases and chances of the mental process" (originally: „Trauern. Phasen und Chancen des psychischen Prozesses"), from the psychotherapist Verena Kast from Switzerland. Today these works are outdated (Nestmann, 2007b, p. 1140).

The American psychologist William Worden has laid down today's standards for grief counseling through his approach to grief counseling as growth and development of clients (ibid.). He sets out the main tasks of grief counseling:

> "Worden called four such basic tasks ' (Worden, 1999, p. 19-25):"

- "accept the reality of the loss,
- to experience and process the pain of mourning,
- to adapt an environment, set by the party concerned
- to the dead should be emotionally assigned a new place to be able to trace own life again." (Nestmann, 2007b, p. 1141).

American researchers of the constructivist field have further complemented this model with the following tasks of mourning:

1. **Search for meaning** ("meaning reconstruction, Neimeyer, 2001", quoted in ibid.), difficult events change our understanding of the world. A question of meaning of life and a new understanding of life are therefore essential;

2. **Identify and maintain permanent connections** ("continuing bonds, Klass, 1996", quoted in Nestmann, 2007b, p. 1141) – during war trauma there are relationship losses. The strength to cope with this should be looked for in bonding, possibly with the remaining family members;

3. **To learn and understand the world again** ("relearning the world, Attig, 1996", quoted in Nestmann, 2007b, p. 1141). Traumatic experiences are like the impact of an earthquake on previously held beliefs. Negative results can cause in many cases two extremes – either a completely negative understanding of the world ("all are evil"), or about the self ("I deserved it"). That's why the biblical understanding and sense explanation is balanced and solution-oriented. You can read more about it in the chapter "Life Meaning Work in the Pastoral Care".

2.6.5.4. Practical Help

Migrants and refugees often have problems which they must deal with: language barrier, culture shock (adapting to a new culture and social structure), residence problems, work and existence problems, mental and health burdens, often family crises, and much more. Although they need a trustworthy interlocutor in a counselor, practical help is needed even more. That's why such counseling centers deal with all local services, which is of crucial importance for such people. In this respect, the recommendation of positive psychology to deal with all supporting institutions is very necessary and practical. The same applies to pastoral work. Very often such services are the work of social workers at competent war trauma centers. In the case of a private practice, cooperation with a competent social center is recommended.

2.6.6. Life Meaning Work in Pastoral Care

Very often, people with war trauma have experienced a loss of meaning, hope and faith. They cannot understand what is the meaning of their life, when they have lost everything through the experience of war. Very often, the whole personality is attacked by the experience of violence, humiliation and loss of worth. Religious people have an additional problem that is expressed by an oft-repeated question: "Where is God? Why did he not prevent that?" Because this issue is very often misunderstood, many people lose their trust in God and in other people and reject even their entire faith and become strong skeptics and critics of faith (Nestmann, 2007b).

The task of pastoral care among such traumatized people is to help sufferers to regain the hope, that God offers his help and support us in this unjust life struggle and one day, when Jesus comes again, a new world will be created for us, where injustice will forever pass away and be removed.

A very important role in pastoral care is to give meaning to, and a sense of, life. The associated method is called "Sense work" (Klessmann, 2008). It is also important to give a reasonable explanation and meaning of suffering generally, so that clients can see that God does not leave them in the lurch, and that their life is not lost (see the following chapter). This is the object of "logo-therapy" called "Sinnzentrierte Psychotherapie" ["sense centered psychotherapy"] from Dr. Viktor Frankl, as its founder (Frankl, 2010). The research of positive psychology has seen this as an important task too (Seligman, 2007).

A reasonable and acceptable life sense and life meaning can be of great importance and great help in the life of the traumatized people. This is, however, a very big challenge for any pastor or counselor, to explain reasonably the meaning of suffering. Religious people often have the serious problem in the matter of the sovereignty of God and its relation to their case. The standardized logic assumption that God is responsible for everything and nothing can be done without his permission is often asked: "If the Almighty Father is good and caring, why does he allow that bad things that affect also the innocent? Where was he then?" – these questions are asked particularly by those affected by injustice, humiliation and violence. The worst and disastrous answer would be: "It was the will of God", because God is always against injustice. The entire Bible bears witness to that. There is more about this in the next chapter.

It is important to clarify to spiritual oriented clients, that this world does not work according to the will of God, because it was originally quite different – it was created as absolute perfection.[52] Here happens a **sense reconstruction**. The next chapter discusses all important moments in relation to this issue.

Resilience improving: Though God needs no defense, it is important to help the clients not to feel rejected and abandoned by God, but to understand that God suffers with them and he accompanies them in grief (Isaiah 63:8.9).[53] Also the need and sense for justice are important. Many suffering people wonder why God does not punish injustice, but very often allows evildoers to go unpunished. The result is not only a feeling of powerlessness, but very often exasperation and disappointment. This is why their negative mental situation may lead very often to deep depression.

---

[52] Genesis 1,31 „And God saw everything that he had made, and behold, it was very good. And there was evening and there was morning, the sixth day" (English Standard Version, cited from http://biblia.com/books/esv/Ge1.31 on Mai 21, 2014).

[53] Isaiah 63:8 For he said, "Surely they are my people, children who will not deal falsely." And he became their Savior. 9 In all their affliction he was afflicted, and the angel of his presence saved them; in his love and in his pity he redeemed them; he lifted them up and carried them all the days of old. (English Standard Version, cited from: http://biblia.com/books/esv/Is63.8 am 13.05.2014).

Theodicy – question why God permits the suffering.
The work in the area of life meaning is noteworthy (Seligman, 2007), to understand better the issue of injustice. Jesus Christ is the answer. In him the whole injustice of this world is condemned and punished – he took the sins of all human beings on himself and so destroyed them in the cosmic dimension by his own death as the bearer of all sins (Isaiah 53:5-8)[54]. He condemned any injustice through his own death (Romans 8:3)[55] and also experienced even the wrath of God against every injustice (Galatians 3:13)[56]. It is also important to emphasize the righteousness of God through his judgment court and to its restoration in the time of the second coming of Christi (Revelation 22:12)[57].

---

[54] Isaiah 53:5 But he was pierced for our transgressions; he was crushed for our iniquities; upon him was the chastisement that brought us peace, and with his wounds we are healed. 6 All we like sheep have gone astray; we have turned—every one—to his own way; and the Lord has laid on him the iniquity of us all. 7 He was oppressed, and he was afflicted, yet he opened not his mouth; like a lamb that is led to the slaughter, and like a sheep that before its shearers is silent, so he opened not his mouth. 8 By oppression and judgment he was taken away; and as for his generation, who considered that he was cut off out of the land of the living, stricken for the transgression of my people?" (English Standard Version, cited from: http://biblia.com/books/esv/Is53.5 on 14.05.2014).

[55] Romans 8:3 "For God has done what the law, weakened by the flesh, could not do. By sending his own Son in the likeness of sinful flesh and for sin, he condemned sin in the flesh," (English Standard Version, cited from: http://biblia.com/books/esv/Ro8.3 on 14.05.2014).

[56] Galatians 3:13 "Christ redeemed us from the curse of the law by becoming a curse for us—for it is written, "Cursed is everyone who is hanged on a tree" (English Standard Version, cited from: http://biblia.com/books/esv/Ga3.13 on 14.05.2014).

[57] Revelation 22:12 "Behold, I am coming soon, bringing my recompense

However, this time has not yet come and that's why the true righteousness of God still does not reign on this earth. The question: "why does God allow injustice to prevail?" is question of timing. Everything comes in its time. Now is the age that God has given to humans to reveal themselves completely, undisturbed, as they actually are (age destined for "the man of lawlessness")[58]. Many do not understand that if God would prevent every injustice, no one could actually survive, because we are all unjust before God. Actually, this time of freedom, when everyone has the opportunity to do before God, what he/she wants this is actually his mercy. It is not easy for us, also not for God, but this is the only way to grant full freedom to all humans. To emphasize again: the freedom of the will is sacred to God. Now we practice our human justice that makes us mostly unhappy. However, all suffering people can have the assurance that the absolute righteousness of God will arrive one day, because the ruler of the universe has determined and promised this (Revelation 22:6)[59].

Continued from previous page

---

with me, to repay each one for what he has done" (English Standard Version, cited from: http://biblia.com/books/esv/Re22.12 on 14.05.2014).

[58] 2 Thessalonians 2:3 Let no one deceive you in any way. For that day will not come, unless the rebellion comes first, and **the man of lawlessness** is revealed, the son of destruction, (English Standard Version, cited from: http://biblia.com/books/esv/2Th2.3 on 14.05.2014).

[59] Revelation 22:6 And he said to me, "These words are trustworthy and true. And the Lord, the God of the spirits of the prophets, has sent his angel to show his servants what must soon take place." (English Standard Version, cited from: http://biblia.com/books/esv/Re22.6 on 14.05.2014).

It is also very helpful to strengthen the hope of victims that God can create something new from our suffering, as well now and as well as in the future. Even in this life, he can strengthen us and continue to bless us. It was confirmed through the research into resilience and the trauma growth. The future new world is also a solid promise about this (Revelation 21:5)[60]. Confidence in the heavenly Father and the hope that he gives us, provides a new perspective which can help grieving people.

It is necessary to clarify that there is no general satisfactory sense explanation for all experiences of each individual. Every case and every person is different. It is therefore important to look for the meaning of their lives sensitively and actively together with the clients (Klessmann, 2008).

Senselessness of injustice. Furthermore, it is important to prepare the clients that injustice has no sense and no meaningful explanation. If a reasonable explanation for every suffering exists, then it would be correct and not unfair. Futility is also a part of life. Fatal accidents, wars, diseases have no rational sense – people feel that as unfair (Klessmann, 2008), because it is really the case. The injustice is pointless per se and may never make sense, nor can be justified. Only what makes sense and that is understandable, although often

---

[60] Revelation 22:5 "And night will be no more. They will need no light of lamp or sun, for the Lord God will be their light, and they will reign forever and ever" (English Standard Version, cited from: http://biblia.com/books/esv/Re22.5 on 14.05.2014).

terrible, are natural consequences of errors or injustice of the perpetrators, which predominantly affect the innocents.

Why God condones injustice? The explanation why God condones injustice lies in the freedom and responsibility, which God has given humans. According to the Bible, God has created man as a free being, who has freedom not only to choose good, but also evil. Each suffering and trauma is often a short- or long-term consequence of false human action. Finally, the whole negative reality of this sinful world is the result of human choices and not of decisions by God.

The most difficult problem with traumatic experiences, particularly with the war trauma, is the question of the justice of God in suffering (theodicy) (Klessmann, 2008). War-traumatized people have serious problems with the meaning of life, because their life foundations and their world are destroyed (family, values and identity loss). For this reason, sense work is very valuable to repair the affected sense of life. This is the firm and most important basis of resilience, as well as of personal trauma growth. When **spiritual questions arise**, it is important to hold onto the following facts, which cannot be changed by any suffering or injustice:

2.6.6.1. The Bible about Injustice, Suffering and Death

The following basic ideas can help clients to comprehend the difficult problem of the suffering and the trauma from the standpoint of the universal, biblical perspective:

1. According to the Bible, the main cause of injustice and of the death are the Devil (John 8:44) and his fallen angels (Revelation 12:9) who perform the evil through them on obedient humans (2 Timothy 2:26);

2. People are originally created in the image of God as perfect – without faults (Genesis 1:26.27; 5:1; Ecclesiastes 7:29);

3. Each person is, on the basis of the creation, a child of God and therefore infinitely valuable for God (John 1:12; Psalm 8:6);

4. God and his reign are absolutely good – without error or traces of evil (Psalm 31:20; Exodus 34:6);

5. From God, we get only the positive and the best – he takes care of everyone (Matthew 6:25-32) and leads people on the right paths (Psalm 73:23.24; Jeremiah 29:11);

6. He gives his help where it is needed (Psalm 20:2.3), when someone asks him (John 16:24; Hebrew 4:16);

7. Actually, the unlimited permission for the domination of evil was given by the first human married couple, at the beginning of the history of mankind (Genesis 3:17-19; Romans 5:12).

8. Responsibility for evil lies not on God, but on humans, because they have got the complete rule (hence also the full responsibility) over this Earth from God (Genesis 1:26-28).

9. Since humans wanted to rule on Earth no longer according to the will of God, but according to the will of the snake – of Satan (according to the principle of "sin"), everything is developed from that as the whole of human

history tells us: wars, hate, murders and destruction come in the whole package of evil, what our first parents have decided. The consequences were inevitable (Genesis Ch. 3). The contract with Satan became valid with two consents (of Adam and Eve) and therefore irrevocably.

10. God allows injustice and suffering, because he has given to us humans free will and free choice of our destiny (Genesis 2:3), but he helps and comforts us in our suffering (2 Corinthians1:2.4);

11. Jesus has shown through his terrible suffering, that only he can bear and overcome suffering, grief and sins of all people (Hebrew 4:15.16);

12. His sacrifice and suffering are the way to a better future, a model for all people – through the victory over suffering and sin to the glory (1 Peter 2:21; 4:12.13), which he is now preparing through his intercession service in heaven (Hebrew 9:27.28);

13. This hope on the Second Coming of Christ and a new world, where a perfect justice reigns, is absolutely safe and trustworthy (John 14:1-3.10.11; Revelation 22:6).

2.6.6.2. Influence of Faith on (War) Therapy

Stronger confidence and hope is developed in sufferers by the therapy/counseling/pastoral care, the stronger and faster resilience and the posttraumatic growth become – to discover the power of God, the courage, the hope and love through their own potential and to activate these in their lives. Through a positive belief, all the noblest virtues can be developed to support mental and spiritual resilience and growth, similar as in positive psychology. In a successful case of a counseling process victory over the done evil develops and also an alteration of bad effects of trauma instead of transfer of evil by implants from the offender to the victim (introjection).

The following ideas can help clients to achieve a higher sense of life and to comprehend the complete context and perspective of the question of evil, suffering and injustice.

2.6.6.3. Ideas about the Higher Meaning of Life and Suffering:

1. Original life sense. Upon the Bible, humans are created as perfectly good, after the image of God, to live forever in a loving community with each other and with God, and to reign over all the Earth (Genesis 1:26-28; Psalm 8:5-9).

2. Cosmic war against God. As free being with free will, the loftiest and most beautiful angel Lucifer (Hebrew "Hellel" – Isaiah 14:12) has rebelled and tried to replace the rule of God over the whole universe through his list and rebellion (Isaiah 14:13). By his opposition, he has seduced a third of the heavenly angels and brought them to Earth (Revelation 12:4);

3. Taking over of the dominion over Earth. Through the seduction of the first humans Satan took over the dominion over the Earth and transformed its people into slaves of sin and evil (John 8:34). This rule takeover allowed him, as to the new representative of the planet Earth, again the access to the heavenly Council and God (Job 1:6; 2:1).

4. Cosmic dimension of evil. From the book of Job (chapters 1 and 2) it is clear that Satan has advertised his idea before all the "sons of God" and thus wanted to spread its influence over the entire universe. From this disclosure, it is clear that Satan has fought the entire universe and that the battle between good and evil has cosmic dimensions, which complicates the whole issue on Earth.

5. Significant change. By the wrong decision of the first people in choosing Satan as the ruler, evil, injustice and death became dominant forces on this Earth – the inescapable curse over all the Earth (Genesis 3:17-19);

6. Universal character of evil. By the self-chosen fall, all humans become sinful and evil (Romans 3:23; 5:12) and hence the whole of this world turns out to be infected by evil (1 John 5:19);

7. The new law of the human nature. Through the change in human nature (»sin fall«), evil has become a universal law of this life and so of all humans (Romans 7:14-21.23.24) who are carnally minded (Romans 8:5-8);

8. God's solution for the liberation of the people from evil. To release people from the dominion of sin and of Satan, Jesus has taken over the debt and the punishment of all people on himself (Isaiah 53:4.6; Hebrew 9:28) to give each man his divine righteousness (Galatians 3:13); so the death of Jesus gives to each human who believes in him victory over their own evil (1 Corinthians 15:57);

9. Final victory in the universe. Thus, Jesus has defeated forever the power and dominion of rulers of evil throughout the whole universe and limited them only to this earth (where they have already taken control over humans) (Revelation 12:7-12);

10. The true justice. Only through his salvation, Jesus gives his true (altruistic) righteousness (Romans 5:18-21) and thus the true victory over evil (John 8:36; 1 John 5:4.5); thus we become righteous without guilt (Romans 3:21-26);

11. The Earth – the combat field. This life and our earth are the last field of the cosmic struggle between good and evil, between Christ and Satan, where Jesus shall defeat evil forever (Colossians 2:15; Revelation 12:10);

12. The final victory in the future. By the victory over evil, now in his own life and at his second coming to all believers, Jesus Christ gives eternal life and thus the rule with him in eternity (Daniel 7:27; Revelation 2:7.11.26; 3,5.21; 20.4; 21.7; 22,5);

13. Higher sense of suffering. On the basis of the whole Bible it is plausible that life with all its sufferings and struggles with evil is a preparation for the rule with Christ – as Jesus has defeated evil, so can all his believers feel it as well in their own and get to know it in all its facets and finally defeat it (1 Peter 2:19-25). In such a manner are the redeemed glorified and rule with Christ over the whole universe in eternity (Ephesians 3:9-12; Revelation 22:5).

On the basis of all these considerations, it means that every unfortunate and traumatic experience, on the one hand is a result of evil in humans. On the other hand they are opportunities for us to grow, to be spiritually mature and to be a conqueror with Christ over evil. It is the ultimate goal of God, that even these victorious experiences qualify us to be experts on evil in the whole universe for all eternity. Through our own genuinely successful experiences with sin we become able to warn intelligent inhabitants on other planets against it as a potential principle and so to protect them, so that in this way the history of fall in sin is never repeated in the universe.

3. CRITIQUE OF POSITIVE PSYCHOLOGY

Although positive psychology has made a positive contribution to psychology, psychotherapy, counseling and pastoral care, it is not acceptable uncritically, because it can make no claim to exactness. It has a good approach in the area of psychological "immunization", but not with regard to the diagnosis of disorders or diseases. The "clinical" side of the disease- or disorder diagnosis is also very important. In positive psychology the personal story has no great importance as a diagnosis tool as in clinical psychology / psychotherapy. Therefore you cannot handle everything only with positive psychology in therapy / counseling.

In the understanding of the human nature, positive psychology is partly approximate to biblical anthropology – despite all weaknesses, everyone has also his / her positive resources which he / she can invest in positive ethical and life values. According to the Bible, all good gifts come from God, since he gave them to every person through their creation / birth and through the Holy Spirit (inspiration). Positive character traits in positive psychology are compatible very clearly with the Christian ones – you can find six virtues with twenty-four strengths (see entire table on the page 48) directly and indirectly in the Bible, but, for that, more space would be necessary (such an analysis is recommended). Above all, a positive attitude towards life, to do good out of selfless love, is the highest motive in both approaches.

In contrast to many psychological fields of study, positive psychology emphasizes a very important area in life, that is basic in the Christian pastoral care – spirituality / transcendence. Although the vast majority of practitioners of positive psychology are declared atheists, they have discovered through many empirical researches that spirituality is an enormously important part of life, which is a strong scientific confirmation and support for the Christian pastoral care. It is natural, that you can't find a deeper explanation what spirituality in positive psychology means, because it is not possible for such a thing. Caution in relation to the concept of "Transcendence" is needed, because, in positive psychology, it is not necessarily something to do with the supernatural (e.g. with God).

I recommend further studies that would optimally integrate positive psychology with Christian pastoral care because of similarities in social and therapeutic areas. During my research, and looking for sources, I found no such studies, which would have incorporated both approaches, which therefore requires a further research area. This work is therefore to propose a pioneering project with the intention of further developments in this direction.

Positive psychology is quite compatible with Christian pastoral care in the field of human emotional and ethical nature. In the social and natural sciences fields (neurobiology, genetics, chemistry, etc.) both approaches go in the same direction, to meet the needs for a positive change in the inner values and positive life style that improve the life quality. Nevertheless, in terms of explaining the meaning and purpose of the formation and development of the emotional or psychological structures of the human nervous system, positive psychology is based on the idea of the evolutionist development (which is allegedly constantly moving in a positive direction). According to this idea, humans can reveal themselves and therefore needs no supernatural force from outside. According to positive psychology, humans have already positive qualities in their genes and their personal development (Fredrickson, 2011). Subsequently (allegedly) evolution goes anyway in a positive direction (which in reality is, only reflected in the technical and scientific field, but not globally on the ethical one) and humans continue to develop further until one day the whole of humanity will be better. On the top of this development is, according to Seligman, God – a godlike character (Seligman, 2007). In his opinion this is not a supernatural, omnipotent God, but a level of character development as a perfect role model for the whole of humanity.

For all Christian ministers, who accept theistic evolution as development philosophy, that is no problem. According to this view, identical to the understanding of practitioners of positive psychology, God is not the omniscient, omnipotent creator of the universe (Seligman, 2007). Because this world has still many errors, it seems as if evolution is still in progress. That's why this idea sounds acceptable for many scientists, as well as for the liberal theologians and is in line with the modern scientific understanding of the origin of the world. Therefore the view of the theistic evolution is a compromise between faith and science.[61] But for the Christian counselors who accept the biblical creation[62] as a basis for their own life philosophy and their counseling praxis and consequently the salvation through Jesus Christ as the only way of healing of souls, the background idea of positive psychology about the world evolution and self-development is unacceptable. In this respect, this idea is typically evolutionist and somehow esoteric (development to a divine level). Therefore, this moment should be carefully handled and separated from biblical Christian understanding.

The same applies to the understanding of human nature. Positive psychology assumes it from the humanistic idea, that man is completely good and that all problems happen only because of the incorrect development of the social and emotional value system of a person. Supposedly, all of these problems can be corrected by treatment involving positive psychology. There are also various pastoral views –

---

[61] According to the theistic evolution widely accepted in the Christian world, God has not created our world in six literal days (each of 24 hours), but in six long evolutions periods, much like as in the atheistic evolution – in billions of years. In some directions of this theory, God was not directly active, but has only controlled development processes (Wikipedia, 2013). This concept comes from the idea that one has to understand the Bible not literally, but only symbolically, especially when it comes to the moments, which are contrary to the modern science.

[62] According to the Bible, man is not a product of some long development process of continuous improvements, but is created through a perfect creation in the image of God, just as a "finished product" of the perfect creator (Genesis 1:31). His current condition is far away from this original perfection through the fall in sin and can be restored only through the redemption and re-creation (spiritual in this life and physical by the second coming of Christ).

for some, that's true, but according to the Bible, not completely.

For the Bible-based pastoral care concepts, however, the biblical idea, that the whole world, and every man, is alienated through sin from God and the real life with him (Galatians 1:4; James 4:4; 1 John 2:16; 5:19) applies also to human nature, that is loaded with all sinful (negative) values (John 8:34; Romans 5:12), of which the person should be healed and be set free (Psalm 32:1; John 8:36).

All experts should be aware of these differences to avoid mixing different assumptions. According to the biblical concept everyone needs reconciliation with God, with his fellow human beings (with the exception of people for whom this is not possible) and with him-/herself. This includes also the positive change of the whole personality and of life with its process of value development, where values of positive psychology can be very well (but selectively) combined with Christian ones. According to the Bible, a long-lasting and deep motivation and character change may result only with the help of the Almighty God, through his Holy Spirit, through cooperation with humans. Especially in the case of trauma and war trauma, the wounds to the soul are often so deep that no one, neither therapist nor consultant, can cure them. For this purpose, a divine creative act is necessary. That is why a **successful** therapy or counseling is actually cooperation with God in a process of healing and renewal. Only then, the whole process can function as a true healing or therapy for a client. Finally, the complete restoration and deliverance from all consequences of bad experiences shall be accomplished only through the Second Coming of Christ – through transformation of the body of living ones or resurrection of the dead ones.

Within this study of the subject of trauma and war trauma therapy it seems to me that due to me accessible sources, a complete and detailed concept of trauma management, or a specific therapy in positive psychology is lacking. Basic concepts and results are available, but a more specific systematization is necessary, at least here in Europe. In the case of further interest, there is possibility of exploring this further and more deeply through special studies at one of the universities with studies in positive psychologies in the USA.

4. Formulation of the Hypothesis

After all the submitted materials about war trauma, about positive psychology and Christian counseling / pastoral care, a resulting hypothesis could be formulated on the following manner:

1. An **integrative concept** can lead to a comprehensive approach. For this reason, further research and development is required in the direction of merging of clinical and positive psychology. It is of paramount importance to create a balanced therapy/counseling approach to complement both components – clinical and positive psychology; to integrate war trauma such as PTSD with posttraumatic growth (PTG) and resilience. This is already being gradually recognized in the highest therapeutic circles (Reddemann, 2007).

2. Because the empirical researches in positive psychology (together with all pioneer work of predecessors and resource-oriented approaches) show that this positive approach to the issue of trauma and war trauma makes a good contribution, I recommend building an **integration of the positive psychology with Christian pastoral care** in a new common therapy or counseling concept in a selective and critical manner. This could be named, for example, "Positive Christian Psychology" (Hakney, 2007), or "Positive Christian Therapy/Counseling" (which is not present yet). Therefore, more researching is necessary. Both concepts (or eventually a corporate one) can be very effectively used in psychotherapy

or counseling to help traumatized people to overcome their trauma in a positive manner with the development of resilience and personal post-traumatic growth and together with the Christian faith. A detailed joint trauma therapy concept is yet to develop, for which there is not enough space in this work. Further research is recommended.

3. A further, recommendation of this work is that **the social structures at the systemic level** should be improved, or new ones should be created to give even better contribution to the treatment of war-traumatized people. This can not only bring great benefits for those affected, but also make a good contribution to the stability and prosperity of the whole of society. People, who have overcome war trauma in a positive and constructive manner, are the best stability factors in a society against violence and hatred towards other nations. Moreover, such people can offer the best help and support to other war-traumatized people. How they could be involved in teamwork and to be engaged as helpers in the integration process is the recommendation for further research and structure.

4. For these reasons, I recommend the establishment of the working group of therapists and ministers who can develop an integrated and functional approach from the above-mentioned disciplines.

5. SUMMARY

Positive psychology is plausible for war-traumatized people, because it is not occupied only with negative moments (with experiences of war and war trauma) as in clinical psychotherapy, which often leads to a re-trauma and cause hindrances in further development. Positive psychology works with several constructive approaches, which create a new perspective on life, new positive and constructive view of the world and also positive values that make the whole of life healthier and happier. It is the work on the »internal immune system«, that protects people from negative mental disorders. This is confirmed by the studies presented in this work. This is a good addition to clinical psychology, but not a substitute for it. For this reason, it is recommended to integrate these two approaches to obtain both components for a good outcome – good diagnosis- and good solution-oriented therapy. With combining this integrated approach with positive Christian pastoral care, success could increase, because a reasonable life sense and spiritual component (life philosophy, forgiveness, understanding the question of injustice, higher sense of life, hope, etc.) create the most important life basis for every person. The proposed studies have shown it. This combined, positive, resource-oriented, systemic therapy or counseling can successfully give back courage, hope and strength to many migrant people, who already suffer from a double trauma, to make a new beginning and can be thus a blessing for themselves, their family and society.

This work is more an encouragement for a systematization of a new therapeutic approach – only a pioneer work in the direction of the (not yet existing) common concept of positive psychology, clinical psychology and Christian pastoral care in war trauma therapy, but as well as in general counseling or psychotherapy. A detailed common approach to such therapy is recommended for further development in a syncretism of those three approaches to create a systematic structure of this new combined therapy/counseling.

I am available for possible cooperation or consultation. For personal contact, I'm accessible at the following email address:

     seelsorge_und_beratung@hotmail.de

OATH DECLARATION

Herewith I affirm that: I personally wrote this research paper and I have quoted all used aids and used no other than these specified resources.

Date: 30.07.2012

Signature:

D. Mirković

BIBLIOGRAPHY

1. Albrecht, K. (2001, März 15). Folgen von Kriegserfahrungen für Kinder und Jugendliche. *Hausarbeit im Fachgebiet Psychopathologie des Kindes- und Jugendalters* . Zürich, Schweiz: Grün Verlag GmbH.

2. Athanassoulis, N. (2004, 08. 28). *Virtue Ethics.* Retrieved 04. 10, 2012, from Internet Encyclopedia of Phllosophy: http://www.iep.utm.edu/virtue/

3. AWMF – Fachgesellschaften. (2011, September). S3 - LEITLINIE POSTTRAUMATISCHE BELASTUNGSSTÖRUNG ICD 10: F 43.1. Aachen: Euregio-Institut für Psychosomatik und Psychotraumatologie.

4. Bauer, W. (1971). *Griechisch-Deutsches Wörterbuch.* Berlin: Walter de Gruyter & Co.

5. Benson, H. (1998). *Staying Healthy in a Stressful World.* Retrieved 04. 16, 2012, from Body&Soul: http://www.pbs.org/bodyandsoul/218/benson.htm

6. Bibliographisches Institut GmbH. (2012). *Extroversion.* Retrieved 06. 12, 2012, from Duden Online: http://www.duden.de/rechtschreibung/Extraversion

7. Bundes Psychotherapeuten Kammer. (2012, 04. 08). *PTBS-Risiko in Afghanistan sechs bis zehnfach erhöht.* Retrieved 04. 30, 2012, from BundesPsychotherapeutenKammer:

http://www.bptk.de/aktuell/einzelseite/artikel/ptbs-risiko.html

8. Bundeszentrale für politische Bildung. (2003). *Aus Politik und Zeitgesschichte.* Bonn: Bundeszentrale für politische Bildung.

9. Christian Association for Psychological Studies. (2010, 04. 15). The Abundant Life. *Christian Faith and the Positive Psychologie (Konferenz Broschüre)* . Kansas City: Christian Association for Psychological Studies.

10. Clinton, T., & Hawkins, R. (2011). *The Popular Encyclopedia of Christian Counseling.* Eugene, Oregon: Harvest House Publishers.

11. Collins, G. (2012, 11. 23). *Christian Coaching.* Retrieved 06. 17, 2012, from Positive Psychology: http://christiancoachingmag.com/?p=1099

12. Csikszentmihalyi, M. (1993). *Flow - das Geheimnis des Glücks, 3. Auflage.* Stutgart: Klett-Cotta.

13. Dietrich, M. (2012). Allgemeine Beratung, Psychotherapie und Seelsorge. *Entstehungsgeschichte, Konzept und Ausbildung* . (F. BTS Fachgesellschaft für Psychologie und Seelsorge gGmbH, Ed.) Freudenstadt, Deutschland.

14. dpa/Demography. (2005, 03. 23). *Wunderdroge Religion.* Retrieved 04. 16, 2012, from Focus Online: http://www.focus.de/gesundheit/gesundleben/vorsorge/news/gestaerkte-abwehr_aid_92862.html

15. Elviva.de. (2010). *Endorphine - die Glückshormone.* Retrieved 12. 20, 2010, from http://www.ellviva.de/Liebe/Sex-Endorphine.html

16. Ermann, M. (2003, November). Wir Kriegskinder. *Vortrag im Südwestrundfunk* . München: Ludwig-Maximilians-Universität München.

17. Evangelischer Regionalverband Frankfurt am Main. (2012). *Evangelisches Zentrum für Beratung und Therapie am Weißen Stein.* Retrieved 06. 28, 2012, from Evangelische Kirche Frankfurt am Main: http://www.frankfurtevangelisch.de/zentrum-fuer-beratung-und-therapie-am-weissen-stein-347.html

18. Fischer, C. (2007). *Chemische/Elektrische Synapsen; Biologiekurs Klasse 12.* Retrieved 06. 15, 2012, from http://www.egbeck.de/skripten/12/bs12-31.htm

19. Fredrickson, B. L. (2011). *Die Macht der guten Gefühle.* Frankfurt am Main: Campus Verlag GmbH.

20. Froh, J. J. (2004, Mai/Juni). The History of Positive Psychology: Truth To Be Told. (F. o. Association, Ed.) *Psychologist, NYS* , 18-20.

21. Gehring, C. (2010). *Posttraumatische Belastungsstörungen.* Aue: Klinik für Psychiatrie und Psychotherapie.

22. Gestrich, C. (2005, 05. 08). Kriegskinder aus dem 2. Weltkrieg. *Rede anläßlich des Befreiungsfestes am 60. Jahrestag der Befreiung vom NS-Regime in der KZ - Gedenkstätte Oberer Kuhberg* . Ulm.

23. Govi-Verlag. (2012). *Kuschelhormon Oxytocin.* Retrieved 09. 24, 2012, from Pharmazeutische Zeitung online: http://www.pharmazeutische-zeitung.de/index.php?id=36679.

24. Hakney, C. H. (2007). POSSIBILITIES FOR A CHRISTIAN POSITIVE PSYCHOLOGY. (R. S. University, Ed.) *Journal of Psychology and Theology Vol. 35, No. 3* , pp. 211-221.

25. Herbst, M. (1999). Seelsorge zwischen biblisch - theologischer und therapeutischer Kompetenz. *Vorlesung WS 1998/99* . Greifswald.

26. Huhn, G. (2011). *Flow, Das Geheimnis des Glücks.* Die Flow Akademie.

27. IFA- Institut für Arbeitsschutz der Deutschen Gesetzlichen Unfallversicherungen. (2005, 07. 15). *Phenethylamin.* Retrieved 05. 28, 2012, from GESTIS-Stoffdatenbank: http://gestis.itrust.de/nxt/gateway.dll?f=templates&fn=default.htm&vid=gestisdeu:sdbdeu

28. IRP-HSG. (2012). *Gewalt, Trauma und Glaubwürdigkeit / Violence, Traumatismes et Crédibilité.* Retrieved 05. 20, 2012, from Institut für Rechtswissenschaft und Rechtspraxis (IRP-HSG): http://www.irp.unisg.ch/de/Weiterbildung/Tagungen/Gewalt+und+Trauma.aspx

29. Joseph, S., & Linley, P. (2008). *Trauma, Recovery, and Growth: Positive Psychological Perspectives on Posttraumatic Stres* (1 ed.). John Wiley & Sons, Inc.

30. Jossen, A. (2007). Sequentielle Traumatisierung bei MigrantInnen. *Vortrag* . Bern: Universitäre Psychiatrische Dienste Bern (UPD).

31. Klessmann, M. (2008). *Seelsorge, Ein Lehrbuch.* Neukirchen-Vluyn: Neukirchener Verlag.

32. Koinonia. (2011, 11. 22). *Conference Announcement: Towards a Christian Positive Psychology.* Retrieved 06. 17, 2012, from Koinonia: http://palamas.info/conference-announcement-towards-a-christian-positive-psychology/

33. Kramer, S., & Birnbaum, R. (2009, 02. 04). *Kriegstrauma: Bilder, die nicht vergehen wollen.* Retrieved 06. 26, 2012, from Der Tagesspiegel Deutschland: http://www.tagesspiegel.de/politik/deutschland/behandl ungszentrum-kriegstrauma-bilder-die-nicht-vergehen-wollen/1435212.html

34. Kroll, H.-P. (2012, 04. 07). *www.depression-therapie-forschung.de.* Retrieved 06. 04, 2012, from http://www.depression-therapie-forschung.de/

35. Landolt, M. A., & Hensel, T. (2008). Grundlagen der Traumatherapie. In M. A. Landolt, & T. Hensel, *Traumatherapie bei Kindern und Jugendlichen* (pp. 11-22). Göttingen: Hogrefe Verlag GmbH & Co. KG.

36. Lanfranchi, A. (2004, 10. 01). Kinder aus Kriegsgebieten in europäischen Einwanderungsländern, Trauma, Flucht, Schule und Therapie. *V. Europäisches Kongress für Familientherapie und Systemische Praxis, Berlin .* Berlin.

37. Lehnen-Beyel, I. (2005, 08. 24). *Glaube versetzt Endorphine.* Retrieved 08. 05, 2012, from Bild der Wissensschaft: http://www.wissenschaft.de/wissenschaft/news/256791. html

38. Lopez, S. J., & Snyder, C. (2011). *Handbook of Positive Psychologie.* Oxford: Oxford University Press.

39. Lukas, E. (2011, 10. 27). Langfassung: Dr. Elisabeth Lukas im Gespräch über Logotherapie. (M. Oort, Interviewer)

40. *Luther-Bibel.* (1996). Stuttgart: Deutsche Bibelgesellschaft.

41. Mediaprint infoverlag GmbH. (2004, Januar). *Patienten mit Panikattacken fehlen Rezeptoren im Gehirn.* Retrieved 05. 17, 2012, from Klinikinfo.de: http://www.klinikinfo.de/artikel/viewer-test2.cfm?do=30&site=2&id=18&aid=2450

42. Medmonitor GmbH & Co. KG. (2008, 10. 20). *Stresshormone: Cortisol und Co.* Retrieved 06. 04, 2012, from medmonitor: http://www.medmonitor.de/cms/praevention-stress-bewaeltigen-stresshormone

43. Michels Kliniken. (2008). Posttraumatische Belastungsstörungen. In M. Kliniken (Ed.), *DAS MAGAZIN DER MICHELS KLINIKEN. Ausgabe 03*, pp. 3-20. Berlin: Michels Kliniken.

44. Missler, M. (2003, 06. 27). *So kommunizieren Nervenzellen miteinander.* Retrieved 05. 27, 2012, from uni-protokolle.de: http://www.uni-protokolle.de/nachrichten/id/19365/

45. Mohr, D. m. (2010). *Reform-Rundschau.* Retrieved Dezember 18, 2010, from Dopamin: http://www.reform-

rundschau.de/archiv/article/Dopamin%20-
%20der%20Schluessel%20zum%20gluecklichen.htm

46. Naumann, K. (2009, 03. 27). *Kriegstrauma und Zivilgesellschaft*. (D. u. GmbH, Editor) Retrieved 04. 26, 2012, from Frankfurter Rundschau: http://www.fr-online.de/einsatz-in-afghanistan/traumatisierte-soldaten-kriegstrauma-und-zivilgesellschaft,1477334,2710000.html

47. Nestmann, F. (2007). *Das Handbuch der Beratung 1* (Vol. 1). Tübingen: dgvt-Verlag.

48. Ohe, G. v. (2010, März). *Serotonin, ein wichtiger Botenstoff – Eine neue Studie zeigt den Einfluss auf das Stillen*. Retrieved 05. 23, 2012, from Verband der Europäischer Laktationsvereinen: www.velb.org/deutsch/docs/studie-zu-serotonin.pdf

49. Passow, S. (2005, August). *Traumazentrierte Psychotherapie*. Retrieved 06. 21, 2012, from Psychotherapie & Psychosomatik Silvia Pasow: http://www.passow-psychotherapie.com/dateien/trauma.htm

50. Positive Psychology Center. (2007). *Positive Psychology Faculty at Universities*. Retrieved 06. 17, 2012, from http://www.ppc.sas.upenn.edu/ppfaculty.htm

51. Regensy University. (2010). *Regency University & Seminary*. Retrieved 06. 17, 2012, from http://www.regencyu.org/

52. Scherer, B., Stocker, K., Rottensteiner, V., & Beck, C. (2011, 08. 08). Posttraumatisches Wachstum. *Power Point Vortrag* .

53. Seidler, G. H., Freyberger, H. J., & Maercker, A. (2011). *Handbuch der Psychotraumatologie.* Stuttgart: Klett-Cotta.

54. Seligman, M., & Steen, T. A. (2005, August). Positive Psychology Progress. *American Psychologist* , pp. 410-421.

55. Utsch, M. (2011, 12. 26). *Hilft Glauben heilen? Die Bedeutung des Gebets.* Retrieved 04. 16, 2012, from psychophysik.com: http://www.psychophysik.com/html/re-0752-glaube-heilung.html

56. Wikipedia. (2012, 05. 03). *Big Five (Psychologie).* Retrieved 05. 05, 2012, from Wikipedia: http://de.wikipedia.org/wiki/Big_Five_(Psychologie)

57. Wikipedia. (2007, 02. 12). *Bindungstheorie.* Retrieved 02. 19, 2014, from http://de.wikipedia.org/wiki/Bindungstheorie

58. Wikipedia. (2012, 03. 31). *Endorphine.* Retrieved 05. 24, 2012, from Wikipedia: http://de.wikipedia.org/wiki/Endorphine

59. Wikipedia. (2014, April 26). *Extraversion and introversion.* Retrieved May 01, 2014, from Wikipedia: http://en.wikipedia.org/wiki/Extraversion_and_introversion#Extraversion

60. Wikipedia. (2012, 03. 17). *Mihály Csíkszentmihályi.*
Retrieved 03. 19, 2012, from Wikipedia:
http://de.wikipedia.org/wiki/Mihály_Csíkszentmihályi

61. Wikipedia. (2012, 05. 12). *Noradrenalin.* Retrieved 05.
25, 2012, from Wikipedia:
http://de.wikipedia.org/wiki/Noradrenalin

62. Wikipedia. (2012, 02. 24). *Phenetyhilamin.* Retrieved
05. 28, 2012, from Wikipedia:
http://de.wikipedia.org/wiki/Phenethylamin

63. Wikipedia. (2011, 07. 18). *Positive Psychologie.*
Retrieved 11. 07, 2011, from Wikipedia:
http://de.wikipedia.org/wiki/Positive_Psychologie

64. Wikipedia. (2011, 09. 12). *Raymond D. Fowler.*
Retrieved 03. 19, 2011, from Wikipedia:
http://en.wikipedia.org/wiki/Raymond_D._Fowler

65. Wikipedia. (2010, 10. 25). *Serotonin.* Retrieved 05. 27,
2012, from Wikipedia:
http://de.wikipedia.org/wiki/Serotonin

66. Wikipedia. (2012, 02. 19). *Stresshormone.* Retrieved
06. 18, 2012, from
http://de.wikipedia.org/wiki/Stresshormone

67. Wikipedia. (2012, 05. 14). *Synapse.* Retrieved 05. 17,
2012, from Wikipedia:
http://de.wikipedia.org/wiki/Synapse

68. Wikipedia. (2013, 10. 09). *Theistische Evolution.*
Retrieved 03. 07, 2014, from Wikipedia:
http://de.wikipedia.org/wiki/Theistische_Evolution

69. Wikipedia. (2012, 05. 02). *Vesikel (Biologie)*. Retrieved 05. 17, 2012, from Wikipedia: http://de.wikipedia.org/wiki/Vesikel_(Biologie)

70. Wikipedia. (2012, 03. 24). *Viktor Frankl*. Retrieved 04. 15, 2012, from Wikipedia: http://de.wikipedia.org/wiki/Viktor_Frankl

71. Wikipeida. (2012, 04. 23). *Oxytocin.* Retrieved 05. 23, 2012, from Wikipedia: http://de.wikipedia.org/wiki/Oxytocin

72. World Health Organization. (2011). *Psychological first aid: Guide for field workers.* Genv: World Health Organization .

73. Zöllner, T., Calhoun, L., & Tedeschi, R. (2006). Trauma und persönliches Wachstum. In R. Maercker, & A. Maercker, *Psychotherapie der posttraumatischen Belastungsstörungen* (pp. 36-42). Stuttgart: Thieme.

74. Zahlner, U. (2008, 09. 21). *Fachartikel Trauma.* Retrieved 02. 05, 2012, from Magister Urlike Zahlner: www.uzahlner.at/artikel-trauma.pdf

LIST OF FIGURES

www.ingramcontent.com/pod-product-compliance
Lightning Source LLC
Chambersburg PA
CBHW060257290526
45789CB00001B/346